S0-EGF-464

A Poisoned Egg Blooms

A Memoir

Rose Leuty

Copyright © 2014 Rose Leuty
All rights reserved.

ISBN-10: 0615882595
ISBN-13: 9780615882598

Library of Congress Control Number: 2013916743
Ms. Rose E. Leuty, Nevada City, CA

Dedicated to the brave and real

Anna Ong

1949-2012

Author's Notes

Many of the places, names and identifying characteristics of this memoir have been changed. Quotes are used to heighten the content of this book, but are not to be considered absolute dialogue.

Acknowledgments

Special thanks go to

Sue Villarreal planted a seed in the depth of me to then fertilize it with the quiet power of truth.

Maire Bernhardt shared her expertise in the art of words with compassion and empathy.

Lynn McClain challenged me and never failed to give me a "hug" at the end of her long lists of suggestions.

Roman Zahir jolted my memory of our life and times in the 70s.

A refined and generous young artist of whom I regret to say I don't have a name. In the mid-70s he gifted me with the drawing of my foot.

Create Space an Amazon Company for their assistance in bringing this book to print and beyond.

Fortitude in women is often mistaken for derangement.

Part One

Sometimes I lived in the dark other times I saw too much.

The nudist camps were "resorts" a term Rose's parents used when explaining their whereabouts to Mother's mom, Mimi, and the neighbors to describe where they were on weekends.

The nudist camps were located in wooded out of the way places, down long dirt roads and in deep valleys. They were well kept except for the visitors that chose to extend their welcome by littering up the place and refusing to leave. Trailers were parked in designated areas. A live-in manager, a swimming pool, a volleyball court, a snack bar, rentable cabins and tent spaces were available for a price. The days were full of organized sporting events. Square dance classes and card games in the evenings kept everyone occupied.

At one of the nudist camps they went to as a family, Rose's father was manipulated by a boy named Luke. He was in his late teens. He had connections to a world Rose's father longed to be a part of.

Most evenings when the day's work was done Father tuned on the classics. He waved his arms around pretending he was David Rose, a well-known orchestra conductor. David Rose and his orchestra was Father's view of a high life far, far away from his demeaning lower class physical labor job. His thick cotton blue-gray shirt and pants were transformed right before our eyes into a black pinstriped silk suit and two-tone shoes.

One blistering hot afternoon, Luke lured Father in with the promise that he would provide him with professional recognition as an orchestra conductor followed by extensive conversations that focused on what Rose could do for Luke. It was 1959. Rose was nine years old.

Rose popped her head out of the swimming pool water's edge to get her breath. She overheard Luke talking in a whisper to her father while they sat around a table drinking beer, "She's pretty enough, but her tomboy ways aren't desirable. I promise you if you allow me to have sex with her as I see fit, in your home, in

3

her bedroom it will calm and control her physical and emotional passions."

Father took the bait. He rose to his feet and scanned the pool. "Rose."

She ducked under-the-water, swam hard and fast to the opposite end of the pool, frantic. "What?"

"Come here. We need to talk."

Head down, Rose slinked by the kids sitting at the far end of the pool.

"Rose, I'd like to introduce you to Luke. Do as he wishes. Make me proud."

Rose jabbed her chin into her chest. Silent, she crept away.

Father was reading books Rose never saw. Talking to people she never met.

He believed she and her brothers would understand the sexual needs of the opposite sex if their genitalia were exposed. He demanded that all their desires stay inside the confines of their home and the nudist camps. Rose and her brother's naked bodies were on display to answer the questions her once prudish minded parents turned inquisitive had.

The value and practice of keeping the bathroom door closed for solitude was not within her father's philosophy. Rose asked to be able to close her bedroom door and the bathroom door to be alone. Her requests for privacy were set aside.

This way of life was completely separate and opposite from Rose's elementary school and neighborhood friends' life styles. She was far too embarrassed to share anything that she felt, heard or saw when she was at the nudist camps or home.

Her friends asked what she was doing on weekends, but all she could get out of her demoralized being was, "Oh it's just a resort. We swim, play volleyball and hang out. No big deal."

What was a big deal was keeping the secret. Rose hated it. She was ashamed and angry; moreover, her idealistic and naive spirit didn't want to believe what was right before her eyes.

Long before she knew of Luke, Mother's desire for him drove her to entice him. At the nudist camps she snuck glances, rubbed up against him, caressed his face, hugged him long and hard and invited him into their home.

One afternoon, Rose rushed back to the house to leave off her school books, pick up her roller-skates and then meet up with her very best friend, Mary. She flew into the house. Luke stumbled out of her parent's bedroom and into the living room, shimming his pants over his hips and then fumbled while buttoning his shirt over his hairless chest. Speechless, Mother stayed in the bedroom.

Rose ran past Luke to her bedroom, grabbed her skates, made a quick reverse, glared into his eyes, ignored her mother lying naked on the bed and then left.

That same weekend at the nudist camp, Rose saw Luke and her forty-five year old mother walk into a cluster of trees only to return hours later laughing, caressing each other's butt. Their cheeks flushed when anyone spoke to them.

Months later, Rose's mother supported Luke's access to Rose's body. For all she knew Mother never questioned his desires for her only daughter. If Mother did, Rose suspected, Luke would stop giving her what she wanted from him. Rose's heart was crushed. She sought refuge in her room with her cat, Tuxedo. His warmth and purr soothed the emotional pain long left over when Luke was out of sight.

In disbelief that her own parents thought so little of her, she made one last attempt to stop what was about to happen to her. But Father and Mother stated, "They won't believe you. You're just a kid. Luke assured us that in time you'd want it," when Rose stood quivering at their bedroom door threatening to tell a teacher, a friend or a neighbor.

Rose couldn't find the strength to step outside the power that her parents had over her. She had no one to believe in or who believed that she didn't want that man in her life. Shame stuck inside Rose's spirit. Her friends backed away. They didn't know or understand why their once open and enthusiastic friend turned glum. Lost and alone, she gave in.

Luke always had a cheap gift to feed Rose's shattered heart. Her need to fulfill her subservient role in order to appease her guardians made her able to be manipulated.

Rose's little bedroom neat and tidy, full of pretty things that she had received from her grandmother, Mimi, and her collection of glass and ceramic animals that she had bought with her own money was overshadowed. One afternoon when Rose was visiting her best friend, Mary, a double bed was pulled and hoisted out of the guest room behind the garage to replace her twin bed.

It was Mary's birthday and Rose was so excited to be invited to Mary's lovely home. Mary's mom had decorated their big fancy living room. Balloons and streamers filled the space. A huge center table was loaded with presents just for Mary. Games and prizes and kids galore made Rose's day a joy.

Beaming with excitement, she ran home wanting so very much to share all the great news with her family, but when she ran into her living room not a word from her was allowed.

Mother stated, "We have a surprise. Go to your room. Luke needs room to move."

Rose climbed onto the huge bed. It dominated the space. She screamed inside, "Where in the hell is my bed."

Whenever Luke wanted her, Rose had to perform the forced act of sex. "No" made no difference. Yelling at the top of her lungs made no difference. The neighbors could hear her, but no one told her.

Law enforcement came by saying that there was a report of a "disturbance of the peace" coming from this address. Promises were made to quiet down. It lasted a while. Then the fights seeped back into Rose's home. Rose was desperate to say something to those men in blue, but she could only watch from behind a chair. Her throat clenched tight. Even if she was asked to tell her truth it would put her life in jeopardy.

Wanting to forget the secrets, physical pain and shame of her life at home, on her way to and from school she sang, "Sticks and stone can break my bones, but words can never hurt me," over and over again struggling to move forward every single step to her fourth grade classes into the sixth grade. She tried with all her heart to believe the words, but loving words don't love when force is the seed that has poisoned them. She made herself forget what happened every time Luke walked into her life. There was no other way to live.

An unfamiliar moist sticky weighted feeling dripped down onto her panties. She tiptoed to the toilet pulled her pants down and then sat on the toilet.

Years before on a rare occasion Mother had sat down with Rose. They shared a book that explained the function of the male and female body parts with pictures and medical terminology in graphic detail. A kit in Rose's dresser drawer that included a dozen Kotex pads and a sweet calendar was ready. But this was not a book full of pictures.

"Mom.....come here.....I need you."

"Why."

"Maaaaaaaaaam........... Come here."

Open handed, Rose presented a thick dark-red blood stained wad of toilet paper and then whispered her demand, "Look."

"So, you started your period, big deal."

Wide-eyed and shaky Rose tightened up.

Mother let out, "Rose has just entered a new phase in her life."

Father heard the news. He paraded into the bathroom, kneeled down on his knees, hugged his one and only pre-teen daughter and then boasted, "You're a woman, congratulations," bowing to Rose as if she were royalty.

Mother, cold and direct stated, "The box in your drawer, read it."

Within minutes, Luke heard the news over the phone.

Mother was so excited she could hardly speak, "He wants to marry you, move into the guest room behind the garage and produce children. He wants you to be his."

Rose was barely into her so-called bedroom when she made an about face and then forced herself to state, "I don't want to be his. That's nuts. I'm eleven. Luke's twenty-one. He's too old for me. I don't even like him. He gives me the creeps. No one I know gets married when they're eleven. Isn't it against the law or something?"

"Rose, he's a good provider. He wants to take care of you."

Laying face down on the enormous battle field, Rose muffled, "No."

Nonetheless, Mother and Father were ready and willing to sign a consent form as soon as Rose was twelve years old. They could do that.

"You're lucky someone wants to take care of you," Mother said after listening with deaf ears to Rose's pleas to end the madness.

Rose's brothers, Art and Stanley, didn't say a word to her.

The loathing that Rose felt for Luke and her parents ran her life. There was not a moment that went by that her gut wasn't full of anxiety and self-demeaning fantasies. Wherever she walked, the ground was all that she saw.

To sever herself from her family was a goal Rose didn't how to fulfill. Whenever they were on their way out, she made up excuses so she didn't have to go. There was always homework, forgotten chores or at the very last minute she wouldn't jump into the car.

Once alone, she skimmed through the monthly "TV guide" hoping for a Shirley Temple movie, a romantic musical or the Frank Sinatra Show to carry her away into the land of make-believe. She did favor one of her parent's big band LPs, Glenn Miller and His Orchestra. But her favorites were Ricky Nelson and Johnny Crawford of the TV series' "Ozzie & Harriet" and "Rifleman." They were so cute and kind. Rose adored them. Those two shows were packed full of family morals, traditions and set roles foreign to the dysfunctional life Rose was surrounded by. They gave her hope.

If there was no such luck, she'd put on one of the 45s she'd bought with her allowance. It was worth the four weeks of a quarter each week to buy one 45. The song Johnny Crawford sang titled "When I Fall in Love" is the song that taught Rose what love is.

Lyrics: Edward Heyman   Music: Victor Young

> *When I fall in love, it will be forever.*
> *Or I'll never fall in love.*
> *In a restless world like this is,*
> *Love has ended before it's begun.*
> *And too many moonlight kisses,*
> *Seem to cool in the warmth of the sun.*
> *When I give my heart it will be completely,*
> *Or I'll never give my heart.*
> *And the moment I can feel that you feel that way too,*
> *Is when I'll fall in love with you.*
> *When I fall in love, it will be completely,*
> *Or I'll never fall in love.*
> *And the moment I can feel that you feel that way too,*
> *Is when I'll fall in love with you.*

In the cramped, often tension infested living room, Rose sang and danced on top of their 1940's upright piano bench, being who she wanted to be, someone else, anyone else, but who she was. She was a star, on stage and beautiful, expressing the songs she heard of love and hope outside of the prison in which she was encased. Over and over a favorite song eased her sad heart, with her body absorbing the soothing penetration of sound.

While she was lost in her dreams, their 1950 Chevy cloud-gray two-door sedan rolled down the street and up the driveway with Father, Mother and her two brothers in tow. Quickly, Rose turned off the TV or (Hi-Fi) phonograph player and scurried into her bedroom. She lay next to her cat Tuxedo, curled into a ball in the middle of the huge bed. She didn't want to explain. It was her world.

In the spring of 1962, Rose was a twelve years old seventh grader trying, but failing to pull above average test scores. The end of three years of manipulations to do for Luke, beatings if she didn't, hysterical thrashing "NO" turning into silent obedience and the isolation from her friends and neighbors, she had had it.

Rose's fourteen year old brother Art's bedroom was right next door to hers. All along, he could hear her fighting off Luke and not getting anywhere. One afternoon, when they were hanging-out in his bedroom, he whispered soft and true, "You don't have to do that with him. Did you know that?"

Rose's chest hollowed. She shook her head.

"Sis, I've been talking to some friends about what's been happening to you and they know it's wrong."

This was the first time anyone in her family showed the slightest bit of concern for her welfare. No one seemed to give a shit, but now she had an ally.

Minutes later, a trembling, but determined Rose stood up against the feeling that her body wasn't hers anymore. She ran through the living room and passed her parents that were engulfed in their books just inside the front door. She forced the door open, stood outside on the front lawn, turned to face the house and then began yelling hysterically at the top of her lungs, fully aware that the neighbors', with only a single one-lane driveway between her house and theirs, could hear her. She wanted them to. "You are WRONG to allow Luke to have sex with me! He DOESN'T love me! He's taking advantage of us! You want me to marry him. I will NOT marry him! He will NEVER make you famous! He's giving you a bunch of bull. Why can't you see that?"

Father rushed out looked up and down the street grabbed Rose by the shoulders then snarled, "Go inside."

Head up, jaw set she sneered and jammed her fists into her hips. At that very moment, Luke drove up the street and parked in the one and only spot the city allowed them to place their car on the street.

Luke's big, fancy, pink 1958 Cadillac was right in front of their house. Rose hid behind the bushes, but she was ready to repeat her angry words. For a long time, she listened.

Luke was barely out of his car, still on the street. Father revealed a controlled and direct command of himself that Rose had never seen before, "Stop, you promised, you said."

"But Gilbert, give me a little more time. I'm here to see Rose. Let me love her."

"GET OUT OF HERE......................NOW."

Rose could hardly believe her ears.

In the past, when Father questioned Luke's intentions, Luke made every effort to change Father's mind in hopes of getting his way with her one more time, with success. This time he didn't. Luke left.

Rose came and went from the house and school as before, but her spirit was hidden away.

After many lengthy pleas to live elsewhere because the memories were haunting her, they had to face the facts. The embarrassment brought on by Rose's statement of truth was undeniable.

When Rose was thirteen years old, in an attempt to keep their secret involvements behind closed doors, she was moved to Mother's friend Vi's house. A bouncing tennis ball battered from court to court, Rose complied with hope for a better life.

Vi, in her fifties, rented out rooms in her home for supplemental income. As a caregiver, she had been there for Rose's grandmother, Mimi, during her last days. When Mimi was seventy-eight years old and Rose was twelve, Vi found Mimi dead hunched over her desk. She had been writing a letter.

Mimi had never met or known of Luke. Knowing that the dear lady wasn't going to be a part of her life anymore brought great sorrow to Rose's heart.

When I was a little girl, Mimi shared Thanksgiving with us. She came dressed in pearls, hat covered with a veil, gloves, nylons, pumps and a perfectly fitted black dress. She helped me set the table and then demonstrated knowledge of every motion of upper class manners as she gracefully sat down in her chair and began eating slowly, with her napkin and left hand on her lap. I adored sitting next to her. Deeply confused as to how to eat and be proper, I followed her lead.

Rose was not going to forget the gifts that Mimi gave her: eloquence, social ethic, form, quality home décor, cleaning, ironing, laundry, cooking, quiet lady-like gestures, wearing silk night gowns, feminine dresses and nylons, bathing in a claw-foot bath tub and eating strawberries on her porch on hot summer afternoons.

Vi wasn't around much, especially when she had a seventy-two hour shift caring for an elder in their home. But being alone gave Rose the peace and quiet that she cherished. Her room was decorated and furnished to Vi's liking. Rose helped with the chores and every morning before going to her first year of public high school, she had to drink warm lemon water for her health. Vi kept the refrigerator full of food and there were loads of sodas available in the garage. Rose drank far too many while watching soap operas on TV after school and in defiance snuck her first cigarette from a small drawer in the dining room hutch, knowing perfectly well that she would sneak a smoke with her classmate and walking buddy, Linda, the next chance that she got.

Vi received adult-only magazines in the mail that Rose couldn't ignore. They were full of stories about the escapes, affairs, murders and exploits of grownups brought on by greed, jealousy, lust, passion and frustration.

Rose's room and board was paid-in-full by her parents, but they rarely called or came by. The isolation from them fed the shame she had not only for herself, but also for the very people that held her life in their hands.

Vi's other boarder was a drunk. He did not close the bathroom door or flush the toilet after he was done. The smell of his beer-filled urine and feces wafted out the door. He never bothered Rose, talked to her, touched her or acknowledged her presence.

She was on her own, to think and try to figure out what to do and she was so confused.

When home, after all her chores were done, Vi, like Rose, loved to exercise. She did her stretches in the living room in front of the TV. Rose thought it was beautiful how at ease she was with her body. When Vi was a young woman she had been a track star.

One rare evening Vi pulled out a picture album of herself running track with her high school and college teammates to share with Rose.

Browsing through the album Rose said, full of admiration, "Pretty great, Vi. I bet I could do that."

Vi exclaimed, "Sure you could. Try it. I'll come to your track events if I can. I promise. Rose you can do whatever you want to do, but you have to want it so badly that no one can stop you."

When I was five years old my older brother Art, and I biked to the miniature golf course after school. That's what he wanted to do, but I watched, in awe, the little girls dressed in black leotards, pink tights and ballet slippers through the screen door of the local dance studio next door. Longing to belong, but too shy to approach the teachers, I sat wondering what a ballerina's life was like.

Father's cold and narrow perspective, "It's a waste of money. You'll never make a living as a ballet dancer. It's a foolish childish dream," distorted my hopes and wishes.

The early months that Rose lived at Vi's, Linda and she walked, at night, in their neighborhood on the lookout for a date. Linda was a troubled girl. Mother, believing Rose could help others, said that she could steer Linda to a moral path. But Rose had very little direction in that very subject and was completely dumbfounded as to why her mother believed such a thing.

In the late-spring heat of southern California, Linda and Rose were at the end their freshman year of high school. One night, a couple of guys took them up to the hills in their car. Linda and her date were in the back seat having sex.

Rose's date looked at her and then said in a whisper, "Do you know what they are doing?"

With her eyes welling up with tears and shame twisting her gut she whispered, "No."

The teenage boy quietly explained and then to her surprise said, "You are not like Linda. She is a whore and not the kind of person you should be hanging around with."

Rose had absolutely no idea what to say, but he was right. She hated how right he was. She had seen Linda in action. Welcoming boys into her house when her mom was at work.

She watched the boys' parade into her friend's house and then pretending it was OK she waved and then said, "So long, got loads of homework... See you tomorrow."

Rose stopped walking in the evenings with Linda, but because they were friends, she slowly and politely ended their walks to and from school or going to her home. It was hard. She was her friend.

Rose was eternally grateful to that boy, whom she never saw again, for caring enough to express his opinion.

Time was up. Rose was back at home for reasons she was never told. She suspected it was because of the stolen cigarettes, her outings with Linda, but most of all, Father wanted Vi. There was that afternoon when he lured her into her bedroom with the promise of fixing a stuck window. Rose was left in the living room to read. Within minutes, the bedroom door flew open. Father stomped out of the house.

Vi stepped out of her room to state in a whisper the telling tale of Rose's future, "I'm so sorry. It's been really good having you here, not only because of your sincere need to help me out with the household chores, but the company has been endearing. Your parents have to make different arrangements. I can't have your father coming over to, as he put it, help me."

Mother assumed Rose would stay. She, who had been born into an atmosphere of gentility, wanted her girl maid back. Where else would Rose go but home, she figured? "Rose everything will be just fine. You'll see."

It was understood by Mother, but not Rose.

Rose avoided her father. Luke had been banished from their house.

Any chance Art got he lay on the living room floor in front of the TV. He wouldn't allow anyone to change the channel or pick a show to watch without his approval. If anyone got the nerve to question his choice he stood his ground, "You got a problem? Need a knuckle sandwich?" his fist in your face.

Art despised how much his parents deviated from the norm.

One afternoon when Father was still at work, Art stomped into the living room, forced open the 1910 Gunn Co. oak stacking barrister bookshelves Mother had inherited from Mimi. He scooped out her coveted paperback science-fiction books and yelled, "Why can't you be a real mom? Cook for us, clean the house, dad works hard, you lazy bitch."

Mother rushed to his side and flung herself down to the ground, "Stop! These are mine."

Art yelled, "We're your children, not pages of a book. What's wrong with you?" shoving her into the wall then kicking her in the stomach.

His younger brother, Stanley and Rose saw and heard it all, but said nothing. They were too afraid to move, much less say a word. Rose wanted to thrash him something fierce, but she stood frozen.

Petrified, Rose sneaked into her now pretty little bedroom and prayed that Art would leave her alone. He didn't always act this way. Sometimes a yellow rose, her favorite, from their back yard showed up on her dresser after a fight, but she wasn't going to take a chance.

Art's frustration bled into Rose's room. He pulled the door open. Threaten to slam her collection of glass and ceramic animals to the floor if she spoke. Tight as a clam in its shell, she said nothing. It didn't matter. One by one, he picked up her miniature animals, watched her squirm and then he threw them at the wall. She stared at the floor full of her lovely things, some broken, some not. He stomped out. It was her job to clean up his mess.

Stanley never seemed to react to the turmoil of the household. He loved to build structures from blocks and Lincoln Logs. His table always filled to capacity with a project. In the midst of his plan, his focus was great, intent on his world.

With no interruptions, Stanley and Rose returned to their old ways, doing all the chores. Art was much too good for, as he put it, "menial labor."

Mother pampered Stanley. She spoke for him and refused to wait for an answer when he did have an opinion.

In 1952 when I was two years old, Stanley was born with an unusually large head that was compressed during childbirth causing water to accumulate around his brain. A caesarian birth was not suggested by the attending physician. In time, they deeply regretted their lack of experience and strength to choose such an action.

Not long after his birth Mom and Dad didn't appear to notice, but I did. So worried for my little brother, I forced myself to say, "Mom, Stanley is shaking his head a lot. What's wrong?"

"It's nothing."

"But Mom he does it a lot."

"Rose, it's not your concern. Leave it up to me and your daddy."

Not until he was four years old was he taken in to have the fluids that were circling his brain surgically removed. When he arrived home the top of his head and forehead was covered with sterile bandages. He was given my bedroom in which to recover. I had to sleep in the boy's room. I didn't like it one bit, but he was my little brother. I loved him.

No matter what, Stanley and Rose had their connection. When they were no more than five and seven years old they began doing the yard-work. Rose was the boss. She mowed the lawn and he edged it using an unwieldy manual edger. This was followed by her sweeping the grass into piles to put into the garbage cans for pick-up. Then to bring the job to a perfect and tidy end, she'd hose the bits of un-swept grass off the sidewalk and down and out to the street exactly like Father had taught her.

Their very favorite job was the gathering of oranges from the fruit trees in the back yard. They wheel barrowed a load to the house, hand lifted them into the kitchen and then Stanley cleaned them and Rose cut them in half. Using their Mixmaster with the juicer attachment in place, they made delicious fresh squeezed juice for their family. They were so very proud to put gallons of bright orange, full of pulp, juice into the family's refrigerator.

"Look what we did," flowed out of their hearts.

I was cracking.

The responsibilities to keep house, protect and mentor Stanley at home, school or outside in the presence of the neighborhood kids were about to end. Rose had to turn her focus on herself. She couldn't take the unspoken truths and chaos at home. She was trying to keep the house in physical order and attempting to stop the unstoppable battles.

Art needled and browbeat Rose incessantly.

Her will outweighing her size and strength she yelled back, "Stop it, you big bully," pushing his sixteen year old massive muscle-bound body away.

He rammed her into the corner, pinned her down and beat his fists into her back. She curled up tight and trembled. No one stopped him.

Nightly, the entire family was exhausted when Art finally went to bed. They treaded lightly around his bedroom.

In the midnight hour, Rose observed the relationship between Art and Father. She wedged herself behind the doorjamb that led from the hall to the living room. Their parent's bedroom door, now with the desperate need for quiet, was closed, only a wall away from Art and the blaring TV.

Father severely disciplined Art until he was fifteen when he saw it wasn't working. He gave up. Father allowed Art to do much of what he chose, including watching TV until 2am. They had a relationship of unfulfilled love and twisted fear. Art understood Father's weaknesses and used them against him.

Art, smug and loud exclaimed, "You're a dirty old man. You can't get a job worth shit."

Father, in spite of his love for his son or maybe it was because of it, could only say, "We need to get some rest. Go to bed."

The TV continued at full volume until Art chose to go to bed.

When my father was an eight year old boy, one cool rainy night a flash of lightning burnt the retina of his eyes. His ability to be an asset to his father as a farmhand diminished drastically. He had to leave elementary school. He couldn't play sports or read a book. To give him purpose, his mother instructed her only child in the ways of a household servant. It was not until he was twenty-five years old that surgery and the assistance of thick lenses restored his eyesight. It cost the family dear. It never left their hearts.

It was a hot and dry evening when Father and Art got into a heated argument that turned physical. Before then, Art hadn't hit Father. Full of oppressed, seething, uncontrollable anger he turned on his eldest son. A battle broke out. Fists were flying and furniture was slamming into the walls. Father was not going to let up.

By that time, Art, a seventeen year old junior in high school, was a huge specimen of a man with a self-obsessed mind. He could have killed Father, but he left him standing, blood dripping from his nose and mouth, his arms wrapped around his chest, about to fall. Art rummaged through the closet and found Father's coat pocket. Car keys in hand, he glared back at Father, "You're a weak old man," running full-speed to the car, he left.

No one went looking for him. The cops were called, but only after Mother pleaded with Father to find out where he was.

Art was parked not far away in another neighborhood. He was taken to jail, charged with assault and battery and then held for further questioning.

Art declared to a law enforcement officer with the power and will of a man, "If my parents don't get me out of this place, I'll tell you what they made my sister do."

What was held secret could no longer be withheld. Separately, Father, Mother, Art and Rose were questioned. In intimate detail, the questions revolved around the life they led behind the front door.

Rose sat in a dismal concrete room with only a single metal table and chairs on opposite sides. Her sunken shoulders, distorted face, knees clenched under her tight enmeshed fingers; she couldn't image what was about to happen to her. But maybe an end to her oppressive controlled life, the disgrace that hovered over her spirit every waking hour would come to an end.

A clean-cut forty year old portly man wearing a gray suit and black tie cracked opened the door. Upon entering, the smell of his butch-waxed slicked down black hair made Rose want to vomit.

He glared into her eyes, looked up and down her body, shook his head and then announced, "I'm Detective Paterson here to question you in relationship to the alleged rape of yourself by Luke Harvey."

In one swift motion, he pulled out the other chair, switched it backwards, opened his legs wide, straddled the seat and slapped a manila-folder on the table.

Rose cringed and lowered her gaze to her lap.

Now face to face, the detective flipped over a black and white picture of Luke and demanded, "Do you know this man, answer yes or no?"

Rose's lips quivered. She wanted to explain, speak her truth, but her words weren't allowed. She knew too well how not only her words, but her feelings meant little to her parents. Seconds away from being completely inaudible she pushed the answer out, "Yes, but..."

"Answer yes or no."

"Yes."

"Did you have sexual relations with him in your bedroom?"

Rose wanted to scream her answer. To stop all this, to go home, find her cat Tuxedo, curl up in a ball in a corner of her room and nuzzle into its purr and fur, but... This was her chance. "He made me."

Matter-of-factly Detective Paterson said, "Answer yes or no."

A flood of tears dripped onto the cold gray metal table. In terror she whispered, "Yes,"

"Did you like it?"

Rose stammered, "No," her lips quivering all the while thinking, "How could he ask me that? What did Luke, what did Father, what did Mother, what did Art say?"

"He says you did."

Her memories had faded. She had had to do that. They were fogged up in her head, but she knew, "I didn't."

The cold, disbelieving eyes of Detective Paterson pierced into Rose's gut, "Why didn't you?"

In a split second, *Luke's ugly penis pushed hard into her groin,* "It hurt. It hurt a lot."

"Did he want to marry you?"

"Yes."

"Why won't you?"

One more chance to speak her truth, "I don't like him. He gives me the creeps. I won't marry a man I don't love."

Smug and arrogant Detective Paterson stated, "Aren't you too young to know what love is?"

The song "When I Fall in Love" filled her spirit with joy. She whispered, "No."

"Thank you. That will be all."

The Detective lifted himself to his feet, switched the chair back in place under the table, picked up his manila-folder and without any further acknowledgment of Rose in the room he walked out the door.

Rose stumbled out of the room. In a haze she trudged down the hall of the police station. Her parent's and Art's fallen bodies were sitting and waiting on the bench designated for witnesses, getting up only after Rose stood directly over them. Pale and about to faint she followed them to the car.

Down the hall of the court house, but close enough for her to understand, Rose overheard a guard state, "Rose is an emotionally unstable fourteen year old. She shivered in the presence of the detective and then after answering the questions she shrunk into a ball."

Rose was not told what Father, Mother or Art were asked or said.

Unbeknownst to her the lawyers and her parents found a way to falsify the time frame of the rapes to one year instead of three years. Self-serving Mother convinced the lawyers that Stanley being only ten years old was unaffected by the years of turmoil within their home. He was never questioned. Rose knew better. Rose knew the truth, but she kept her mouth shut. She was convinced that not a soul would believe her.

Months later, just outside the courtroom door, Rose waited. Her sweaty palms and tight gut dominated her hopes against the odds that they wouldn't need her on the witness stand. Luke pleaded guilty. She was numb. After sharing a home for fifteen years, her family broke apart. An L. A. county judge determined that the entire family except Mother and Stanley must live apart for one year. Father was charged with misconduct in the presence of minors and child endangerment. Mother was an experienced liar. She got off scot-free. Luke got away with only two years probation, a fine and was handed a no contact order. At that time, within the judicial system, *pedophile* was not a term used as a description for a man or a woman having sex with a child.

Rose couldn't understand how, why, or what gave the adults the right to lie and manipulate her life that way. She hated them all in the silent protected cavern of her mind, but she didn't admit it, not even to herself.

I was never young and untested.

Shattered into pieces one must glue the parts
together to be whole.

In the warming summer days of 1965, Rose's fifty-three year old father and seventeen year old brother Art were living outside the home. Father, an amoral tormented man, had been labeled an unfit father. He was living in an apartment, a designated distance away from the house. Art was attending a military school. Mother hoped he'd learn respect for his fellow man and acquire disciplinary skills. She promised to visit. Rose still had her ally, but the rest of his family didn't want to lay their eyes on him ever again. At fifteen years old, Rose was given the opportunity to attend a Quaker boarding school for her sophomore year. Her thirteen year old younger brother, Stanley, believed unable to survive without his mother, continued to live at home.

Those sizzling summer and fall months, when Rose's mother was fifty-one years old, she regained her independence. A college graduate, she had forgone her ambition to work alongside her father and best friend, James, in the Plant Pathology department of the University of California in Riverside to marry Father. He was an alluring poet and an unrelenting sexy man. He took care of her parent's garden and aspired to own and operate his own nursery "someday." Now, she bought a used 1958 white Chevy station wagon with a dark red interior. Rose couldn't for the life of her remember what she said, but she knew Mother had "a bee in her bonnet" and wanted and needed to feel a sense of freedom. What got into her mother was a mystery to her, but she reveled in the change.

The spunk expressed by Mother, which until then simmered underneath sluggishness, was perplexing to an exuberant little girl turned defiant teenager.

Mother, Stanley and Rose had been living a few months on their own when she needed to be driven to the boarding school in a small town way up north. Her mother was saddled with the obligation to drive her there. Stanley came along. They were familiar with camping and decided Yosemite National Park would be a good midway point between southern California and northern California.

With an air of a once free and adventurous woman Mother said, "This may be our one and only chance to go camping as a trio."

Bound for places Rose had barely or never seen, they loaded up the station wagon with camping gear, changes of clothes for Mother, Stanley and her, plus all the things that had been requested by the boarding school. Mother drove the whole way, but as always, Rose was designated to be the cook, the organizer, the map reader, the traffic watcher and the never ending giver of moral support.

"You can do it. I know you can," Rose pleaded when Mother made the slightest move to put her on the bus and freight her belongings to the school.

They woke up early to beat the traffic. It wasn't bad for the first few hours, but when the trucks going through the Grapevine on their way towards Bakersfield kept passing them by and overtaking them, it became unnerving. Mother always kept in the slow lane and so did the trucks. Wedged between the massive freight packed impatient trucks, Rose was convinced they were not being seen. She couldn't see the drivers so how could they see them? Mother, determined Mother, her focus on getting them to their destination "come-hell or high-water" kept them on the move, the only car sandwiched between endless numbers of overpowering big rigs.

For miles and miles her luggage rubbing up against her thighs Rose kept her eyes peeled for the Merced exit. It was a blessing when she spotted it, the turn off to Yosemite National Park. They made their way, curve after curve, to the magnetic meadows, waterfalls, ski run notched mountains and boulders of the vast national park.

Their campsite was situated under an umbrella of Giant Sequoias. The branches extended from and then wove themselves into one another from the massive trees. The crowns were beyond their sights. The protruding roots cradled Rose's spirit for the very short time she was allowed to be a part of their lives. The cool moist air and soft forgiving soil beneath her feet gave off tranquility unknown to her until that day. To her, it was the biggest cleanest freshest place in the world.

They pitched the canvas standing-room four-sleeper tent. Rose set up the cooking station. Mother and Stanley, as expected, immediately sat down on the lawn chairs and proceeded to read. Rose, also as expected, wanted to and did wander about after a "be very careful, don't go far" from Mother. It was a brand new environment, so beautiful, but very unfamiliar.

Barefooted, Rose treaded into the waving grass outside the campsite, looked up with amazement, gave in to the fatigue, sat down and then lay down surrendering to the tall meadow grass and wildflowers that hid her from view, absorbing the power of nature. It was paradise.

A daydream carried Rose to a fantasy long unfulfilled. A nurturing mother warm and kind calling, "Dinner's ready."

But the growling and emptiness in her stomach rang out. Rose ambled back to the campsite to find Mother and Stanley, as before, sitting and reading waiting for her to make dinner.

There days and nights at Yosemite National Park went by with habits formed long ago at home. All the small chores were orchestrated by Rose and followed by Stanley. Mother and Stanley continued to sit and read with an occasional change of pace when Rose talked Stanley into going for a hike, but most of the time she ventured out alone, farther and farther from the campsite, watchful of her surroundings.

After packing and loading up the car they found their way to Kindle City, a tiny town nestled in the foothills of the Sierra Nevada Mountains. There were no freeways or shopping centers then. Upon arrival, the Live Tree School paperwork was completed. Rose's energized, dutiful mother had fulfilled her task.

The secretary asked if Mother and Stanley would like to see the dorm, help her unpack and say their goodbyes in private.

Mother's response, "We need to get back on the road. She'll only be here a year," sucked the breath out of her.

Stiff and detached Mother and Rose hugged and then straight and to the point Mother said, "Don't forget to write."

"I won't."

Stanley, without a word, hung his head.

The white Chevy station wagon with a dark red interior ascended up the hill soon to disappear like dandelion fluff. Rose stood in the office doorway suitcases at her feet, sad but relieved.

Her room and roommate had been assigned, but she hadn't arrived. After unpacking Rose meandered around the building that was to be the stage for yet another life's worth of dramas. Just down the hall from her room was the upstairs bathroom. Walking in she noticed the row of stalls, went inside one, closed the door, sat down on the toilet, cupped her face with her hands and began to weep. She had privacy. No one was going to walk in, start to wash his or her hands, take a bath, stand in the doorway glaring at her or demand that she hurry up. The stall was hers. There was a lock on the door, a real lock that she could use if she chose. She used it even though there was no one in the bathroom or wandering about the upstairs of the dormitory. Sitting on the pot in the stall sobbing, she realized that she didn't have to relieve herself right away. She was accustomed to quickly taking care of business. The idea that she could sit there in private was a shock, a revelation and a miracle to her. She lived so differently from her friends. Their bathrooms were decorated in lovely floral wallpaper and smelled of perfume, scented soap and candles. She couldn't share her shame with anyone, but Rose never forgot.

When I was seven years old a second grader, it had become difficult to feel then act on my body's signals. The odor I feared all could smell and the weight between my legs frightened me to the core. If I was home alone, I took off my underwear and flushed the mess down the toilet. But most of the time, desperate to hide my elimination, I buried the evidence, first in my closet and then I transferred them to a corner of the garage when no one was looking. My mother would ask me why I had so little underwear to add to the laundry, but she never delved into my vague answers.

Then one afternoon, when I was eight years old a third grader, my parents decided to straighten up a corner of the garage. Looking through my bedroom window, I saw what they were doing. My throat, jaw and face froze in terror. I paced within the tight space between my bed and dresser. There was no one to go to for answers, or anywhere to run to for help.

"Rose, come here this minute." Father yelled.

My legs were rubber, barely able to hold me upright. I wobbled to the back door then hinged it open just enough to peer out the crack.

"Are these yours?"

"Yes," in a whisper.

"Come here."

Then to my surprise Mother said, "Gilbert, let me talk to her. Rose, go to your room."

Watching every move they made, I overheard Mother declare to Father, "Girls need their privacy. Let her close the door."

Mother and I went to my bedroom and then sat on my bed, "Rose, your father has odd-ball ideas. I don't agree with them, but he's my husband. I can't change what he believes. Free-thinking open-minded morals have consumed his behavior, but I did convince him to let you close the bathroom door from now on. I'm sorry I don't have the strength to do more."

From that day forward, I fostered an underlying self-loathing coupled with an anxious fighting spirit hidden deep within.

The almost brand new, community oriented, Quaker boarding school was surrounded by tall pines and oak trees. It housed sixty students and ten staff members. The south-fork of the Sweet River was only a few hours walk away. It was a peaceful place to be.

Fall had turned into winter. It seemed that everyone but Rose got care packages from home. No one was as aware of the lack of letters and phone calls and Christmas invitations as she. Christmas vacation at the school went on and on, but the few people roaming about brought a comfort, not loneliness, to replace the pain and void.

Michael, the principal's son, so handsome, a musician, athletic, an excellent student and responsible person, thought Rose was the prettiest girl on campus. His father was also the P.E. teacher. He led his team of well-trained pubescent boys all around the nearby countryside to high schools in the neighboring counties to compete in the basketball, baseball or flag football. Michael was the best.

Rose would tag along. She loved being a self-proclaimed cheerleader for them all. One night after an exhilarating basketball game they came back to the campus in an old Chevy flatbed truck with wobbly wooden side panels. Huddled together under wool blankets, Michael and Rose found their way to their first kiss. The eyes of their classmates who "knew" they'd inevitably merge watched their bodies slip closer and closer as the truck rumbled up, down and sideways on the poorly maintained mountain road. They hugged and kissed the whole way back. That night Michael and Rose became an institution.

The budding wildflowers and new oak tree leaves were a gift to Rose. She was about to turn sixteen, but Michael was full of himself all week. Not a word about her birthday. She was oddly disturbed seeing how attentive he was most of the time. She was cautious, curious and afraid that his heart had wandered.

The night of Rose's birthday Michael and she met up with their friends at his parent's house to watch the only TV on campus. She opened the door to a dimmed study. Surprise, surprise there was a big white cake with chocolate frosting, her favorite, and presents just for her sitting on the little table in front of the TV. Sweet and passionate Michael presented her with a dark red candle.

Rose said, "I thought you forgot," smiling an adoring smile, but so very close to tears.

"There's no way I'd forget your birthday. We wanted it to be a surprise."

The tears were unstoppable. Rolling down her cheeks uncontrollably Rose whispered into his ear soft and true, "It sure was."

The very next day, a package addressed to her lay on her bed. In haste, she tired to tear it apart believing all the letters she had sent asking for much needed warm clothes and much more were inside. She was never warm enough except in Michael's arms that cold foothill winter.

The package was a big cardboard box. It was meant to be used to ship oranges from southern California eastward, but Father had a way of snatching up boxes for his use. It was taped so damn securely. Rose had to borrow a carving knife from the dining hall to pry it open.

A huge, silly bright pink card, undoubtedly from Father, was right on the top. Secondhand clothes from the neighborhood thrift stores were cramped together and folded with great care, most likely Father's doing. It was obvious that her specific written requests in multiple letters were not acknowledged. The sizes ranged from fourteen to eighteen. Nothing matched. Her now love of cotton and wool made her sad--not at all happy with the polyester tops and pants. Rose was five feet and six inches tall and a hefty 150 lbs. by then and knew her size. The clothes weren't warm enough for the teethchattering winter that had just past. But under the clothes was Mother's dad's wool blanket. The blanket he'd taken on his travels overseas. Thick and scratchy but oh so very warm, Rose wrapped it around herself and paraded it throughout the dorm. She slept under it until it was so hot at night that she couldn't stand it.

When I was no more than five years old, Mother said, one of the few times that we sat together on the couch looking at her family's album, "You're so much like my father," with sparkle in her eyes, "not only in build, but his generous soul and independent spirit are a part of you."

Hidden inside my heart I could tell how much she missed him.

That spring Michael and Rose were inseparable. They walked hand-in-hand to all their classes, did chores for their community, studied, played baseball and made out under the old oak tree that marked the left field, line drive boundary. Whenever Rose was feeling down Michael presented her with a sweet bouquet of cat's ears. He was there to lend a helping hand with her studies. They were the "couple" on campus. According to all those who aspired to believe, they were the perfect duet.

After begging letters proclaiming her innermost feelings, "I love this school. I love Michael. He's the greatest guy. He's amazing. I'm so happy here. Please, oh please let me come back next year and the next," her parents gave in.

During Michael's and her summer apart they wrote daily. His tender precise letters expressed a deep undying love, "I miss you terribly. The walk to and from the dorm is empty. I feel your hand in mine then it's gone. I think of you every minute of every day."

But youth didn't imply a lack of experience of the world nor the human heart. Rose's secrets oozed their way into their relationship. When seemingly all the other guys were having sex because that's what you do, Rose wouldn't, not even when her roommate and Michael planned and arranged an hour alone in her room for them to have sex. The minute Rose saw his penis she clammed up.

Their family backgrounds had a chasm between them that couldn't be bridged. His family was well established in the Quaker Community. As prominent members of the American Friends Service Committee, they were in the process of grooming their son to be the same. Rose felt inadequate for the future Michael might ask her to be a part of. She respected and appreciated his mother's positive, reassuring ways, the English and home economics teacher, but never related well to his aloof father. A lover of babies and possessor of a strong philosophy in the area of family duties, Michael's father and Rose didn't see eye to eye when it came to her future with his son. She was not ready or willing to be saddled with the responsibilities of the offspring which he expected from his son's wife. Moreover, her fears of what Michael would feel knowing that Rose, unlike him, was not a virgin, finally came to a head.

Her first, second and half of her third year at Live Tree School a self-imposed pressure to keep the rape sessions hidden from everyone at the school verged on an obsession. Everyone assumed Rose was a virgin. She didn't care to set them straight.

Making out, as sensual and passionate as Michael and Rose got, was not enough for Michael. Sexual freedom was opening up boundaries Rose had already been forced to extend. She loved being caressed and caressing Michael, but he was full of a young man's needs. Needs Rose didn't fulfill.

Finally one night, sitting in the girl's dormitory social hall with Michael, Rose tried to explain, "There's something I need to tell you. Please don't be mad. I care for you a great deal and believe you do for me, but you don't know about my life before we met. I'm not a virgin. I haven't been for years."

Michael stepped away, stared into her eyes, "You're not!"

"No."

"Then why can't you do it with me. You know how!"

"Yes, but................."

"But what? Why? I don't get it."

"I was raped over and over again. Please try to understand. That's why it's so hard."

Michael's body turned cold, "I need to do it," he stomped out the door.

They didn't break up that night, but his interest, he attentiveness faltered. The walks to and from classes, doing their homework side-by-side in the dinning room, sitting next to each other at meals, making out under the old oak tree waned in slow arduous steps.

Three months later, back from a Christmas visit to her family's home, Rose arrived on campus after another long Greyhound bus trip from southern California. On a pitch black night in January, the tiny registration office light fell over a lone figure at the desk. It was Michael.

The second that she stepped into the office he declared, "Rose, I've been having sex with Julia off campus for months."

To keep the slightest bit of integrity Rose had afloat, she whispered, "I was going to break up with you, but I was going to wait until morning."

Trudging to the dorm, Rose's heart fell to the ground.

There was a rustling from the dorm windows, the doors to the rooms, except hers, shut in quiet haste.

Rose's roommate, the head of a pack of popular young women sat alone crossed legged on her bed. Without even one single second of restraint or consideration for her roommate of two years she belted out, "Did you break up?"

"Yes. You knew?"

"We all knew."

Rose ambled down the short flight of stairs to the bathroom, closed the stall door and then sobbed her sorrow into her hands.

The last three months of her senior year, no boyfriend in tow, Rose flourished in the bosom of the high school as an individual, not encumbered by the principal's son. After two years of asking for a single room she got it. She became a chain-smoker and drank-to-get-drunk on homebrew. She made-out with a couple of boys in the woods and went skinning dipping in the snowmelt waters of Sweet River with the gang to show them.

"I'm no prude."

Not one time did anyone from her family visit her on campus. It was her world without them.

Self-reliance is a gift.

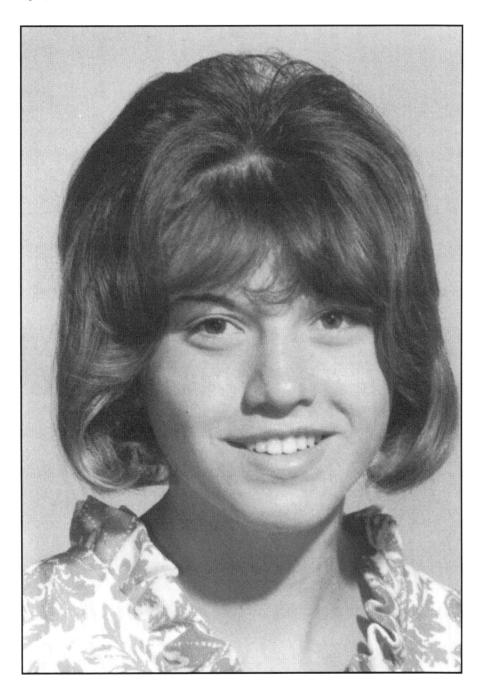

Part Two

In no other situation must your principals be so clearly defined and functioning than during the time of travel.

R.L. Wing

One crystal clear late spring day, Rose, as an eighteen year old high school graduate, crammed herself into a Greyhound bus. It was time to visit her family. After she sat for thirteen hours, unable to sleep or relax, the bus pulled into the Los Angeles bus terminal. Father, Mother and Stanley stood frozen shoulder to shoulder in the mobbed concrete terminal. Rose, surrounded by a fog of fatigue, thought the three people looking straight into her eyes were alien creatures from a world left behind. It was not them that she craved, but freedom. Still Rose couldn't neglect the facts. They were her family.

Mimi left money for Rose to go to college, but most of it was used up paying for boarding school. Mother, the executor of her mother's will, demanded that Rose purchase a car. She didn't think she needed a car. Her attitude was that it was too materialistic. That changed when a used fire engine red 1967 VW Bug at the car dealership caught her eye. It was exactly what Rose wanted.

Mother declared, "I will have nothing to do with a used car. You will only be inheriting someone else's problems," looking at Rose as if she were a fool.

Mother had spoken. Rose ended up with a brand new factory green 1968 manual gearshift VW Bug. She had no say as to what car she got, but what she did with it was her business. In time, she named it Sammy.

The salesman and Rose went for a test drive. She did well, but then she had to drive back to the house by herself. All of the rules of the road that she had ever learned dominated her mind. The one and only manual gearshift vehicle that she drove was an old farm jeep. She pretended that she was in that car, but this was a city full of lots and lots of other cars, traffic lights and angry people, not a long and lonely dirt road going from the barn to the school dorm and dining hall.

Rose said her goodbyes to the salesman with a huge, "Thanks for the lesson," then willed herself to go it alone.

Reassuring he said, "You'll do fine," waving from the showroom floor.

There were quite a number of hills. She stalled the car, got embarrassed, was yelled at, but she made it.

The moment Rose passed through the front door her father, having paid his debt to society, snickered shook his head and then dipped his voice with an all too familiar sarcasm, "You'll never be able to maintain that car."

Rose's father never failed to make her angry. He couldn't support her. It was an impossible task to understand why, but Rose wasn't about to cow-tow to him.

Her gut was churning, but on the surface she glared at him, stood straight and tall and then blurted out the only honest thing that she declared the entire visit, "I'm going to have this car for the rest of my life."

"We'll see," lowering his eyes.

Rose shrunk. *Why in the hell can't he be supportive of me? Why do I care?*

For the next two weeks, Rose engaged in superficial conversations with her family, visited with the neighbors and slept in her childhood's trauma filled bedroom. Her old, squeaky twin bed was back in place. There was no mention of the change. Her parents swept Luke under the rug, but in her groin he never left.

His ghost hinged opened the door, stood over her while she was in bed and then his naked body lingered under the sheets.

For the second summer in a row Live Tree School hired Rose to be one of four cooks for the two-month long summer camp. Self-reliance propelling her spirit, she flexed her jaw muscles, packed the car and drove the first 900 miles in her brand new car to Kindle City.

The cooking job offered a serious but temporary glimpse into the working world. Room and board plus fifty dollars a month nestled in the arms of the school that had given Rose a soft place to fall.

The summer job came to an end. Her two-year relationship with Michael ended with no-goodbyes. The day before she was to leave he didn't have the decency to come to her for a thank you for their time together and a good luck. Rose pretended it didn't matter. Her gentle hurt heart was hidden away.

When Rose drove out of the womb of the boarding school that she called home for three years she was a slim ripe beauty with long, flowing auburn hair, possessing the effortless grace of a tiger, the mind of a hippy-Quaker and the habits of a chain-smoker with no roots and no plans.

Debbie, a former classmate and co-worker needed a ride to Des Moines, Iowa and then to Philadelphia to begin her new life. At nightfall they left in her VW Bug for the long, hot and very boring stretch across Nevada and Utah. The gas price was twenty-three cents a gallon or less. Their money was tight. If they kept the car moving at fifty miles per hour they could cover three hundred miles on one ten gallon tank of gas. Rose and Debbie rationed their cigarette intake to one every sixty miles, bought groceries at the roadside supermarkets, slept at rest stops or stayed at friend's or family member's homes along the way. Rose's mother, worried for her welfare, had sent her some money just in case. She was determined not to use it.

Engulfed in midnight's solitary black hole, a white angelic rabbit sitting straight and tall in the middle of the road caught Rose's eye. She gripped the steering wheel, veered hard and fast, the tires screeched. A sickening smack and then the rolling body deep within the wheel-well sucked the breath out of her. Her eyes welled up with tears. She hung her head. The car slowed to a halt.

Rose whispered, "Debbie, I need to stop."

She belted out, "What's your problem? It's only a rabbit," disinterested in the world behind Rose's eyes.

She brought the car up to speed. Silence filled the tiny car rolling through Nevada.

At 1am, five hours into their journey, they decided to get some shut-eye. The side of the road just past Nevada, in a field off Highway 80, seemed the logical place to bed down.

At daybreak, the darkness that had sheltered them from strangers was gone. They were in plain sight, on the side of the road with out-of-state plates. Rose gagged at the sight of the rabbit's fur and blood that clung to the left wheel-well, but she didn't allow her fears to take over. The freedom of the road, the end of her first love and the escape from his father who was not fond of her independent nature kept her on the move.

For miles and miles the pavement flew under their wheels, the radio blasting the songs of the 60s: Bob Dylan, Joan Baez, Janis Joplin, The Supremes, Crosby, Stills, Nash and Young, the Rolling Stones, Stevie Wonder, Otis Redding, Ray Charles, Chuck Berry, Jefferson Airplane, Country Joe, the Temptations, Martha and the Vandellas. The list goes on. The sheer velocity was exhilarating, but then Debbie and Rose were overtaken by an oppressive looming big rig. Numerous times the driver placed himself directly in front of them and slowed down to a crawl. Peeved, Rose passed the massive vehicle.

Debbie sat shotgun, "He's pointing at the back of your car."

The road had been completely void of another car for miles. Mid-afternoon, hot and dry in the middle of Nebraska, golden prairies of dry grass or corn fields at maturity in all directions, their spirits froze in fear, "What does he want?"

The relentless truck driver compelled Rose into action. She pulled over, but there was no way she was going to turn off the engine. From the rearview mirror she saw him pull over, hinge his truck door open and then saunter in their direction.

In a deliberate, firm voice the medium built well-groomed truck driver said, "Where are you two ladies going?"

"Philadelphia, Pennsylvania," wishing she'd kept her mouth shut.

"You're a long way from home and you have a long way to go."

"Yes, we do," hands on the wheel and ready to gun the motor.

"Please, don't be afraid. I think there's something wrong with your car. Would you please leave your car running and follow me?"

In slow motion, with innards churning Rose forced herself out of the car's womb, but not until she looked to Debbie, "What should I do?"

After multiple lightening-speed glares from Rose to the truck driver and back she responded, "It's your car," fixing her gaze down at her lap and stuffing her hands between her legs.

Powerless, Rose exited. The barren road and smothering asphalt's steam sucked into every pore of her body. She was shaking inside struggling to hold onto her nerves.

The truck driver, standing at a safe distance from her said, "With your permission, I would like to open your deck-lid, then look and listen to your engine."

"O.K., do you think there's something wrong?"

"Yes, I do."

A metal to metal erratic ping immediately got her attention.

"You better get that taken care of. Do you have a warranty?"

"Yes." She climbed back into the car, retrieved the owner's manual from the driver's door-pocket. The closest VW dealer was less than 40 miles away.

Verging on a broken spirit Rose pleaded, "Should I turn off the engine? Would you call a tow-truck?"

Calm as a cucumber the trucker responded, "Better not just yet. That rattle could be a piece of your engine that might settle in the wrong place and seriously damage your car."

His voice softening, "You're in the middle of nowhere. It could be a long time before a certified tow-truck driver can help you. I'd hate to think what he might do to the two of you way out here," calmed her nerves.

It was time for him to retreat from their problem. He had a job to do, "I can't blame you for not wanting to stop. I'm glad you did. I'm running late…It was worth it…Good luck."

Unable to speak beyond a sigh, "Thank you."

The big rig and the hero controlling its destination got back on the road. From the cab he stretched his arm and open hand to them. On their own once again, Rose and Debbie waved goodbye.

After a few brief moments to catch their breath, they checked the map, determined their course of action and were on their way.

The radio off, their minds focused on the rattle in the engine. They prayed for a safe arrival. After many long miles they located the VW dealership safe and sound.

Debbie stayed outside.

Rose held herself erect at the counter of the second VW dealership she'd entered in two months. "My car is making an odd sound. Can you help me?" holding on to every piece of training in the art of pubic relationships that she could muster up.

"We heard," the receptionist acknowledged and then asked, "May I see proof of ownership, your driver's license and the warranty."

Rose knew it was the correct protocol. Before she left home her mother sat her down and offered advice on how to handle oneself in potentially dangerous situations with a new car, out of state, alone and female. Silently, she thanked her.

To the girls' dismay, the mechanics couldn't get to her car until the next day. After being directed to the closest motel and bummed out that their money was going places they hadn't expected, they gave in, they had to. There was no other choice.

Rose and Debbie showered, changed their clothes, ate out at the neighborhood café and endured inquisitive and judgmental looks of disapproval from the locals, "You'd think they never saw a couple of women on their own in their lives."

"It's the car. We stand out like a sore thumb."

Exhausted, they zoned out in front of the TV and then slept the night away.

In the morning, Debbie, smirked, "I'm going to give the maid something to do," shrugged her shoulders lifted her nose to the air and then threw the bedcovers on the floor while the shower continued to run with no one in it.

Rose didn't try to stop her. She simply wanted her car back to fulfill the promise to get Debbie to her friend's apartment in Philadelphia before winter set in.

Back at the VW dealer's reception desk Rose inquired, "What was wrong?"

"A poorly tightened screw shimmied loose. It could have seriously damaged your car. It also needed an oil change and valve adjustment. The warranty covered the cost. You're a couple of lucky ladies."

Nodding and smiling inside and out, Rose responded, "Yes, thank you," and then paced to the car.

Back in shotgun, Debbie ordered, "Let's get the hell out of here."

Rose's introduction into the world of automobile maintenance was a positive one. She was proud of herself and wide awake to the facts. The trucker taking the time to warn them and the mechanics who fixed the problem enabled them to continue.

To be grateful and gracious to all those who help one along the way was a trait embedded in Rose by her grandmother, Mimi. The dear lady's ways were guiding her through Debbie's inconsiderate approach to life.

Rose and Debbie visited Debbie's father in Des Moines, Iowa. To Debbie he was just her dad, divorced, living in a small apartment with the birds and squirrels ready and waiting for a handout, but his generosity put Rose at ease. Debbie and she saw "2001, A Space Odyssey," while they were there. They were awed, but Rose's earthbound ways didn't relate to the futurist mood of the movie.

When the time came for them to move on a part of Rose was left behind in the cozy apartment. They hugged goodbye and at first light left for Hershey, Pennsylvania.

Rose had met Alex from Pennsylvania at the Live Tree school summer camp. He was a striking, long flaming red headed and bearded man, freckled from head to toe, friendly and kind, fulfilling his military duty as a conscientious objector. One hot and dry sunny afternoon when a group of young adults were skinny-dipping in the Sweet River he said, "If you're in my neighborhood stop by."

Rose and Debbie drove to Hershey on their way to Philadelphia. As they drove up to Alex's home the aroma of chocolate from the Hershey factory stirred Rose's appetite. His family welcomed them. To earn her stay, she pierced his sister's earlobes and helped with the daily chores.

Philadelphia was the end of the road for Debbie. They had a problem. How was Debbie going to get from Hershey to her friend's apartment in downtown Philadelphia?

Debbie toyed with the idea of taking a bus, but one afternoon in the backyard when no one was around bold and entitled, she declared, "Rose, I'll take your car."

Flabbergasted that she would assume such a thing Rose exclaimed, "You must be kidding."

"Nope."

"How long do you need it?"

"As long as it takes me to land a job and find a place of my own."

Knitting her eyebrows together Rose demanded, "How long?"

Stomping away Debbie declared, "Rose, I don't know. How in the hell would I know."

Rose cupped her hands over her mouth then mumbled, "What do I tell Alex's parents?"

Debbie turned around, rubbed her lips together hard and tight then shouted out, "Tell them anything. I don't care."

That evening, Rose stumbled into Alex's parent's living room. They were in their easy-chairs reading the newspaper after an excellent dinner that they had prepared.

Beholden to them Rose willed herself to say, "Debbie promised to return my car in a couple of weeks."

She had faked her way through the moment. She had held her head high. That was a lie. The truth was Rose weakened in the presence of overpowering people.

Alex led the way in his truck to the interstate. He hoped they'd come to an agreement, maybe stay at his parents' house a little longer and then Debbie would take the bus. But she wouldn't budge. Dazed, Rose handed Debbie the extra key exited her car and then stumbled over to Alex who was leaning on his truck, "Well?"

"She won't listen to me."

The back of Rose's brand new car was traveling down the road. It was full of the few belongings that she had except for her clothes and toiletries. Stunned and screaming inside, Rose felt like a damn fool. She lifted her arm and waved a meek goodbye. No wave, no honk, nothing came from Debbie.

Alex's family allowed her to stay on until everyone's patience melted into a knowing. Debbie was not going to return Rose's car. Alex needed to visit some friends in Pittsburg before his semester at Eden College in Rex, Indiana was about to begin. They left for Philadelphia to pick up her car. On the way, he invited her to stop by as soon as he was settled in an apartment. They located the apartment where Debbie's friend lived. Rose spotted her car out in the street.

"Rose it's your car. I'll wait."

Keyed-up, gut tight and her heart in her mouth, she knocked.

Debbie swung open the door, "Come on in," friendly as could be.

There was no way Rose was going to even glance at or take one step into Debbie's life.

Stouthearted Rose focused her gaze directly into Debbie's eyes, "Debbie, we need to talk. Why didn't you call, write or bring back my car?"

Sickening sweet she responded, "Rose, come on...I need your car. You agreed to let me use it as long as I needed it."

Rose's heart pounded hard and fast and then rushed up into her throat. Breathing in any air or thought that might end this pain she stated, "Debbie it's my car. I need it right now! Your friends are allowing you to stay in their apartment. The car is all I have. Give me the extra key."

Debbie didn't have it on her and made no attempt to retrieve it.

Rose made an about face, lifting her hand to the sky. When she got back to the street, she was too overwhelmed to spare more than a wave to Alex. It took everything she had left to unlock her car, start the engine and drive off.

Rose was afraid. Debbie had her extra key. Would she in an arrogant rage hunt her down and steal her car, but why?

I was lost in the sea of the unknown.

Unearthed from the people and a place she believed permanent. They had weeded her out. Now, on the other side of the country, miles and miles away from anything familiar, Rose struggled against the temptation to give up.

Through the streets of Philadelphia she wandered aimlessly, except for the fact that she had a flapping piece of paper taped to the dash. It was an invitation and a destination, Alex's place in Rex, Indiana. She had money to get home tucked away in her mobile refuge, the car. Suspended between two choices, she unhinged at the prospect of the walls, the rooms and the life she would enter if she chose that path, her family.

Directions and an address in hand, Rose traveled the distance, killing time in a motel along the way. The duplex was easy to find, but no one was around. It was a week before classes. A note on the door said that the key was just around the corner at the manager's home. There was a decent motel right off the interstate, but Rose longed for personal space.

Ruffled, but with years of practice behind her in the art of deception she proceeded to the manager's home. A nicely dressed man not much older than her opened the door. To the point Rose delivered her need. "Hi, my name is Rose. I'm Alex's friend. He's not at the apartment. He's expecting me. I have no place to stay. I could get a room in a motel, but I'm..."

"Say no more," handing her the keys, "lay low, the gas and electricity isn't due to be turned on for a week."

The alarm that propelled her to the landlord left in a heart beat. Rose's entire body let go of the prolonged tightness.

Filled with gratitude she extended her hand, "Thank you so much."

He responded in kind and then a smile of knowing her need because once he felt the same passed between them.

The apartment's key clutched in the depth of her palm, Rose paced to the locked door, eased the key into its slot and then ever so quietly opened the door. A dismal narrow stairway led up to the stark two bedroom apartment.

Looking carefully up and down the street, she went back to her car double checking that she still had the key. She pulled out her suitcase, blankets and a bag of groceries and then brought them back into the apartment. She didn't unpack, but put her blankets in a corner of the living room, tiptoed into the bathroom, placed her toothbrush into the metal toothbrush holder that extended from the wall just above the sink, opened the empty mirrored cabinet and placed her toothpaste on a shelf, went back to her blankets in the corner. And then she allowed herself to lie down and drift into a deep sleep.

The summer heat was still warm and soothing to her spirit. She waited for Alex.

Kelly, Alex's roommate, arrived first. He was a polite and shy guy, six foot, nineteen years old, tall, lean and bronze from the blistering sun of Texas. An experienced farmhand, he was taking time off from the ranch to get an education.

He wanted to be an engineer. Rose told him her story, at least as much as she wanted him to hear.

His final words, "Let's wait to see what Alex thinks," were a welcome reprieve.

The security of the apartment, a kitchen with running water and Alex's warm and protective feelings for her allowed her to hope, but to feel out of danger was as elusive as an attempt to control the mist.

When Alex arrived, he and Kelly discussed Rose's presence in their lives. They didn't need the living room and figured she could make herself at home for the semester. Wanting to be an asset and not a burden, she proposed an idea. She could pay fifty dollars a month, do the grocery shopping and cook dinner. Alex and Kelly went for it.

Rose decorated the windowed corner of the living room with candles, pictures and an antique cup and saucer set Mimi had given her one afternoon when they had tea on Mimi's porch when Rose was a kid. While the guys were in classes she wandered around campus, checked-out Rex, had an extra key for her car as well as the apartment made for her, bought groceries or did chores. In the evenings she read Herman Hess. Kelly studied. Alex studied, partied and got to know Rose.

Kelly and Rose had a few short-and-sweet conversations. On one occasion when he was taking a break in the kitchen he said, "Very few people would choose to read Hess. He's very philosophical. Good for you. I'm too wrapped up in my homework to be truly appreciative of that man," lowering his gaze, "Got to hit the books."

"Thanks," taken in by his interest, but she held herself back from following him into his room in hopes of getting to know him a little better.

Serious and at times introspective Kelly blushed with embarrassment every time he bit into the chopped carrots nestled inside the dinner salads. Alex and Rose tried not to laugh, but they couldn't help it. One day when she was at the grocery store, she figured it was time to buy a grater. When she unpacked the groceries and set the grader on the kitchen counter Kelly smiled a sweet smile. Nobody laughed at him that night. It was back to the old jokes, the goings-on on campus and Rose's day.

The money Rose's mother had sent her before she left California was hidden away. She had no intentions of using it or letting anyone know she had it. The cash she earned from working at the summer camp was dwindling. Rose needed a job! She bought the local newspaper and perused at the want-ads. *Help Wanted. McDonald's Drive-In. No experience necessary. Will train.* Determined, she jumped into her car and drove straight to the drive-in.

After Rose's polite inquiry the manager said, "Why are you coming to me for a job?"

He looked truly puzzled, but his curiosity gave her hope. She handed him the newspaper.

Nodding, he responded, "Hum, oh yeah, I did put an ad in the paper just last week, but it never occurred to me that a girl would answer it."

A bit unnerved Rose stated, "It doesn't say a word about a girl or boy working," hiding her frustration.

"That's true," drawing out the words, "the guys that have shown up so far weren't much on reliability or guts. You've got guts," smirking, "you gals from California are something else," shaking his head and sighing.

Finally, after numerous questions relating to Rose's experience with the public and reassured of her responsible nature, the manager's response, "I'll try you out. I can pay you minimum wage, one dollar and twenty-five cents an hour. I have a hat. Buy yourself a nurse's uniform and dye it yellow. I'll reimburse you," eased her fears.

In no time, Rose was settled in her new job, but then she received a letter from her mother. Father was about to descend on her world. He loved to travel and whenever he was out of work he would hop on a train just for fun. Out in the world, he was a charming and curious man. The human condition fascinated him. He found great pleasure preaching his beliefs, the beliefs that Rose had stored away in the cave of her memories to survive, to any and all who would listen.

As a child, no more than five years old, I gave in to my dad's flattering ways and my desperate need to please him. I accompanied him to the Winchell's donut shop very early in the morning on his days off. On Saturday and Sunday mornings, I woke to a knock on my bedroom window, the signal that I was to rise and shine and meet him in the kitchen. Daddy, in my idealistic heart, beckoned me as he stood outside of my window, "You're my little girl, come along with me. I'll buy you milk and your favorite donut."

In haste, I dressed and without eating a thing went to the donut shop with my dad, the sun just peeking over the horizon. I was in no state to go anywhere. I needed to be alone, be a kid dreaming my dreams. The weekends were full of chores undone by others. My brothers came to assume that I would complete them for our dad. Getting up in the wee hours of the morning became a dreaded experience, but my dad needed someone to accompany him. No one else wanted to go and I was not accustomed to refusing him.

At the donut shop all the old guys showed up. Dad ordered milk and a cake donut for me, coffee and two of the enormous apple-fritters for himself. Rarely was there a woman. As we all sat around the oval counter that surrounded the grease pit, I became mesmerized watching the baker drop the raw donut dough from a huge machine, one at a time, into the boiling grease. Then when they were ready he turned each donut over with a long handled wooden spoon to brown on the other side. Finally they were removed from the grease, golden brown on both sides and ready to cool on the tall multi-leveled rolling shelf.

In the meantime, Dad went on and on and on, talk, talk and talk some more.

Father wanted to surprise Rose, but Mother knew she didn't want to be caught off-guard after his harsh words the last time she laid eyes on him.

The night after the letter landed on her doorstep, Alex, Kelly and Rose had a few friends over to party. One of Alex's friends had a secret crop of marijuana. He cultivated it among one of the tall fields of corn a mile out of town. They sat on Alex's big billowy pillows surrounding the long-stemmed oriental pipe of a hookah, sucking on the strong mind-altering sweet weed. Rose stared at the smoke as it passed through the container of water humidifying each suck. Their own separate minds took them to the essence of who they were.

After two long inhalations, Rose was drawn into her sensual, sensitive and self-conscious inner world. She had to leave the room. The only room with a door other than her roommate's bedrooms was the bathroom. She plopped down on the toilet, peed, washed her hands and then glanced into the mirror. She took a double-take. Her face was distorted beyond recognition. Her eyes were pulsating.

The pupils were large and black almost completely covering the iris of her eyes. She was petrified. She wobbled to her bed, listened to the others carrying on. Rose couldn't go back in there.

The outside world was not a place she wanted to be. Curled up in the fetal position she thought and thought and thought, "My father will be here in three days. How in the hell am I going to cover up my world? I have a job, but I live in a two bedroom apartment with a couple of guys, I party, smoke two packs of cigarettes a day and suck weed. There's no way he'll be supportive of me, much less sympathetic especially if he finds out that I had sex with Alex when weed or a gin and tonic released my pent up desires."

Why Rose cared what that dirty old man thought was a paradox. On the surface, she was a "who gives a shit," person, but underneath she was the little girl who tagged along when no one else would. She mattered. He needed her.

Rose's education of birth control was vague. After the initial lust had worn off she realized what might be in store for her. She had to. Her period was late.

Friends from work knew of a doctor who was willing to perform a pelvic exam at a discount during off hours. One blazing hot summer sunset, a cloud of naivety hovering over her, Rose entered the doctor's office dimmed lobby through an unlocked dark doorway.

On the edge of anxiety, the doctor completed the exam and then declared, "Your pelvic exam indicates that you may be about to begin the blood flowing stage of your menstrual cycle, or your at the beginning of pregnancy. It's difficult to diagnose at this point. Under no circumstances will I perform an abortion. Go home and try to relax. You may be late because you're nervous. I hope for your sake this is the case."

Lost inside a pocket of questions, Rose drove to the apartment, lay down and prayed. *Please, start, I don't want a baby.*

A few days later the familiar moist feeling between her legs warranted a trip to the bathroom. The usually dreaded blood on her panties rang out the freedom she relished. The anger fed by her childhood traumas didn't allow for the welcoming of motherhood. Rose never told Alex anything. It wasn't his problem. She was no longer receptive to Alex. Her shame and confusion dominated her soul once again.

Every time my period was approaching and then through the heavy blood flow Luke didn't get near me. I wondered if Mother and Father kept him away or was it the sickening red slim that held close to my vagina and disturbed his penetration and then stuck to his penis. I was grateful in the sick pain of my crotch.

Then the pain got God-awful. Yellow puss mixed into the blood. It continued days after my periods were over.

When Luke wanted me I clung to the wall.

Mother took me to the doctors, but only after Luke complained of my refusal to accommodate him. I was eleven years old. I hadn't had a pelvis exam. My parents were too afraid of what they might find out about us.

On my back, legs spread wide open and heels set in stirrups. The female doctor opened me up asked Mother to take a look deep inside my groin.

In even tones the doctor said words I'd never heard of. I could see her sad, but professional expression as she supported my mother to take a closer look at what was happening to me. It was excruciating. I wanted to get the hell out of there. Run to the hills and never go back, but I couldn't. I was stuck.

"Hum," Mother said.

I was stiff, shaking and petrified when the doctor chose to present pictures of mild to moderate cervical infections brought on by rape and poor hygiene. "Your daughter is worse than any of the pictures I have available. She needs antibiotics now and to restrain from any sexual activity that may have brought on this problem followed by surgery. The surgery will consist of burning off the present infected areas."

So cold, so unkind, so matter-a-fact, I could hardly believe my ears when Mother stated, "We'll she ever be able to have children?"

"*Hard to say at this point, it depends on whether or not the infection went up her fallopian tubes to her ovaries. From my findings it may or may not have spread that far. The surgery will determine that. We can do the surgery this month. If she continues to have regular periods after the infection is cleared up the chances of her becoming a mother are good.*"

The morning of the day Rose's father was due to arrive she wrote a note telling him where she worked and to come by. She was about to put it on the front door when she glanced out their second story windows. The figure of a man in his sixties was coming up the walkway to the apartment ten minutes before she went to work. It was him.

Freaked out, Rose gathered her things and then determined to not let him inside she ran down the stairs to the front door.

Fake enthusiasm coupled with blind love she forced out, "Father, you're here! Mother told me you were coming. What a surprise. I have to get to work. Would you like to come along?"

"I'd like to see where you live. How's the car? Can I come in?" attempting to wedge his way up the stairs.

In her heart Rose knew he didn't love her. He hadn't had anything to do with her for years? He was on the move. She was something for him to pass the time, a diversion. Mother said in her letter that he wanted to know how she was doing, but he said lots of things, promised things and had allowed things to happen to her that weren't forgivable much less forgotten.

Nonetheless, Rose politely responded, "I'm fine. The car is fine, but I need to get to work."

"Have you needed to get any work done on the car?"

"Yes, it needed a tune-up. It needs one every three thousand miles," unwilling to divulge the problem with the car in the middle of Nebraska.

She would have loved to share, received his approval of how well she handled herself, but he wouldn't have done such a thing.

Rose's two hundred pound father squeezed himself into her Bug. He had no baggage. It was in a locker at the train station.

For twenty minutes, with great deliberation, his silence looming over her. She maneuvered her car through the neighborhood to the business district. Father's big, rough and powerful hands inches away from her. The smell of his cheap cologne, sweat and a cigar made her want to gag, she said nothing. He stared out the window.

Rose's boss was there and alone, "You're early."

She clocked in, "My father's outside."

"I can't give you time off."

"I'm not asking for time off. In fact that's the last thing I need. I haven't lived with my family for years. I can't stand the man, but he's here."

"Why?"

"He's passing through."

"The rest of the crew will be here any minute. Get things squared away with your father."

False respect pushed Rose outside. Her father stood waiting and watching the world around him. He was an emotionally detached man, unlike her. She couldn't step from one world into another at his speed. Nor did she want to exploit her charm in order to attract prey.

Polite as can be she said, "Would you like to come inside?"

Distant, his response, "I can't. I need to meet the train in an hour," answered her plea.

He went to the counter out front. Counter-girl to customer, that's how she approached the situation. "May I help you please?"

"No, I'd better get going."

As he spoke, Rose saw a stranger, a man she couldn't let herself know, much less love. He was a man who cut into her heart only months ago. Would he again if she ever let him know what she needed from him?

Before my bath, when darkness came to the sky, Dad and I jumped into our almost brand new 1950 Chevy sedan. The car

56

and I were born the same year. Every time I rode in it I felt pretty special, but most of all, I knew I was special when I was alone with my dad on our way to watch the mice families way up in the sky.

Dad opened the door smiling a warm smile, "Ladies first."

I was a four year old girl then. I'd climb into the cushioned seats. Dad followed right after me. He sat down behind the huge steering wheel with the gearshift coming out from the right side of the column. He shifted into reverse then maneuvered the car out onto the street and off we went in search of the moon. I adored my dad. We were a team investigating the goings on of the cheese factory in the ski. Our outings took on a secret togetherness. No one else wanted to go. I was alone with my big brave knowing dad. He was my hero and pal.

I curled up next to him. His thick gray cotton shirt and pants smelled of wood, sweat and oil. I leaned and snuggled up against his strong comforting bulk in the dark, peering out the huge windshield, protected by the warmth of his love. Then we stopped to gaze at the moon and its ever-changing shape. I listened in wonder to the endless wisdom of my dad. He'd tell me tales of the comings and goings of mice living in the sky miles and miles away. They were families making and eating cheese, the food all mice long for.

At the end of its waning cycle when the moon had ever so slowly became only a curved sliver of light. Dad would say with flair, "My, the mice had better open up the cheese factory and begin making more cheese before it runs out!"

Then a few nights later when the waxing moon was on time and began the cycle all over again, a curved sliver of light with a brighter and stronger glow appeared Dad said, "The mice have been working hard the last couple of days. Look how much they have made."

I was completely taken in.

But sometimes I'd question, "How could there be a land so far away? Can they breathe?"

"Of course they can!" Dad stated with great knowing and enthusiasm.

Then, when the moon was full, round and bright I'd ask, "Now that the moon is so big where do all the mice live? It's all cheese. Where are they?"

"Oh, they're resting and eating. They're just too far away for us to see. There are nooks and crannies for them to huddle up in, eat and rest. Can you see the dark spots?"

"Yes?" my head tilted in wonder. I believed him. After all, he was my big, brave, knowing dad.

When we arrived home our story ended. Dad's time was no longer mine until our next outing to watch and wonder how the mice continued with their lives.

Even so, clean and fresh from my bath, under my bed sheets and blanket I couldn't help wondering. But the night grew long. My eyes fell closed. I could no longer daydream of the mice factory way far away in a world full of sparkling patterned stars in a velvet black sky.

As the days went by, I continued to question. My innocent mind worried for the safety of the mice and the story of their cheese factory which was repeated as the only explanation for the waning and waxing of the moon. I'd wonder why some nights the sky was completely black except for a then curve of light and dots in constant shapes throughout the blank canvas of the sky. How did the mice keep from falling off the long straight edge of the half-moon? Why did we need to wait for its arrival and other times find it in our path right away? Why was it sometimes not in the sky at all?

For days and months, when I was small, my dad and I were members of the moon's vast audience. We had a part in the ebbing and flowing of its size, shape and light and an ebbing and flowing of our relationship.

Rose's father lifted a cigar to his mouth, swirled it through the narrow entrance between his lips and then sauntered away. The backside of his bright orange, green and turquoise Hawaiian shirt, pressed gray trousers and tweed jacket hung over his shoulder moved away from where she stood protected behind the counter grinding her teeth. The questions that she feared he would ask Alex and Kelly dissipated with every step that he took. He paused at the bus stop just beyond the parking lot. They got busy. Minutes later she glanced over to an empty bench. Rose was free of him once again.

In no more than four months, Rose had made friends with her fellow employees and received the "Cashier of the Month" award. Then her boss left the district and another replaced him. Women by then were more acceptable as employees. She had started a trend at the Rex Mc Donald's Drive-In that spread throughout Indiana. Nonetheless, her independent nature that gave her the courage to ask for the job in the first place, led her to lose it. When the new boss introduced himself, announced the rules, regulations, salaries and the demands of the job, he handed out the new uniforms.

Stern and reserved, he glared into Rose's eyes, "This is the Midwest not California."

Rose needed the old boss back. She was OK with him, but she tried to fit in. She donned the uniform. She got acquainted with the ladies. She learned of their lifestyles, children, husbands, grand-kids and their assumptions of many, many more to come. They shared menus. She was asked to join their clubs, but declined. She made up stories of her dear family in southern California. That Alex and Kelly were her cousins showing her college life.

Rose's independent ways didn't surface. If they did, she'd be shunned. Questioning authority figures was a part of her. It was time to go.

The frigid winds of winter were descending on Rose's world. Alex and Kelly were leaving. Rose was offered another place to live, but she met, Chad, a California-bound young man. He had family in southern California like her, but unlike her, he wanted to see them.

Their road trip from Indiana to California began the morning after classes ended. A mild snowstorm left the roads leaving town covered with a dusting of snow. The car lost traction on black ice, went into a slow slide and bumped the curb. After a glance at the front right wheel Rose shrugged her shoulders, "No biggy." They were fearless and focused on California.

On Route 66, Rose and Chad encountered a fierce snow-storm. They stopped at a gas station to fuel up and buy some chains. There was a motel nearby, but it had a glowing red neon no-vacancy sign flashing a defeating answer to their needs. The gas station's office was warm and comforting. With a floor that invited temptation to bed-down and wait out the storm. But no offer or request was spoken from either side. The only chains available were too big for the tires. Rose bought them and made do. They had to keep moving through the fierce hard-driving hail and thick snow on the road or freeze to death. For hours the loud rhythmic clang coming from the loose tails of the chains beat against the inner fenders. The snow slammed onto her little VW Bug. They could barely see. They had to open the car door, look down at the road and attempt to follow the lines on the roadway or another vehicle's red tail lights.

Then the wind gave way to a quiet breeze and the skies cleared to a brilliant blue. The snow plough blazed a charcoal asphalt lane pointing the way to their goal. Rose and Chad removed the chains, stopped for a bite to eat then continued on the last leg of their journey.

On the third day of their road-trip, Rose had to tell Chad that she never had any intentions of going home. He couldn't under-stand that the idea of getting caught up in her family's orbit terri-fied her. She didn't know how to explain it, even to herself, much less anyone else. Midnight, they pulled up to a Greyhound bus station one hundred miles from their homes. Chad caught the bus. Rose didn't allow herself to miss him.

By 3am in another motel, she tried to sleep, but couldn't. She needed to get back to the one and only environment which had given her the only taste of long-term peace in her whole life, Live Tree School in Kindle City.

At daybreak, Rose was loading up her car. The manager peered out of the office door, "You just got here. We don't need the room. Get some rest."

A moving target, Rose was unable to receive her kindness and left.

The nine hundred miles from southern California to northern California she was under the influence of a propelled will and sleep deprivation. She didn't stop, she couldn't stop, except to fill the tank and get bites to eat. When the buildings, paths and people of a familiar time came into view the truth of how six months away had suspended her innocent drifting spirit came into the forefront of her mind. She was bound for a place, the only place that she wanted to be.

The school's secretary Mrs. Vale was typing the staff meeting's minutes from last month. She responded with a lovely warm smile to Rose's slow entrance into the office, "Rose, it's good to see you, what brings you back?"

"I'm unsettled, very unsettled, if there's any work for me I'd love to help out. I have nowhere to go and little money. You know how hard I work."

"You're in luck, we're having a staff meeting in a couple of days. There's an empty room in the dorm. Unpack, get some rest and come to the dinning hall for dinner. I'll see you there."

"Thanks ever so much."

After a few days of visiting with old classmates that hadn't graduated yet, helping wherever necessary and loving the rural life, the staff had their meeting. She didn't need to be told. Their faces expressed an unwelcome person among them. With a forlorn heart, Rose accepted there was no place for her in a world that she once loved. Empty and lost she felt once again an orphan. Her need to work there once again wouldn't happen. Michael and his father had made it clear. The other staff members, the farm animals, the meadows and the river had no say.

List in hand of old classmate's addresses and phone numbers Rose drove to Berkeley. After crashing with her old classmates,

Doug and Bob, for a month, Mary offered to share her converted garage, studio apartment, right off University Avenue. It was only a couple of miles from the University of California Berkeley campus. For six months, they pooled their money, shared chores and a space that a single car once occupied. It included a separate kitchenette and a tiny bathroom. They adopted a couple of kittens that caught a life threatening disease that neither of them knew how to reverse. Rose's ignorance of the city feline's health needs opened up guilt-ridden emotions. She had taken in the living creatures, fed them, held them, but they died. All the farm animals she had befriended didn't die the three years she was at Live Tree School, why these. She promised herself she would never experience that again. She vowed to care for any animal that came into her life, as her own, to the best of her abilities.

In the spring of 1969, Rose enrolled at Merritt Jr. College in Oakland. Her focus was on the humanities and creative writing. Cigarettes were her companion, always there to calm her conscience and soothe her lonely heart. She bought a 5-speed black Raleigh bicycle for transportation to and from school, but the long trip across town to school and back brought on chest compression, shortness of breath and pain. Rose's cigarette intake was rearing its ugly head.

One day when she was at school, a hit-and-run driver rammed into her parked car immediately after it collided into an oncoming vehicle at the cross-street. A note from the other victim of the accident led her to the perpetrator of the incident. As warned, she got nowhere when she contacted him for possible payment. He was an uninsured driver and knew he could get away with it. Rose's insurance paid for most of the damage. The mechanics at the body shop discovered the bent wheel-well and axle she unknowingly incurred the first day of her trip from the Midwest. To add to the stack of problems facing her after a semester of classes, her bike was stolen from the alleyway that ran behind the studio to their back door.

In time, Mary and her boyfriend rented an apartment of their own. Rose thrived in the peace and quiet. One late evening, after she'd been on her own for a couple of months, she was sitting cross-legged on a mattress on the floor at the far end of the studio zeroed in on her sociology text book. The streetlight just above her front door was overshadowed by an ominous figure. The back of her neck prickled. Her entire world shrank into a hole of darkness. She looked up to see the silhouettes of three men loitering outside her front door. Ever so slowly she put her book down and crushed her cigarette into the ashtray.

A fidgety figure shoved another away from the door and then declared, "There's nothing worth stealing in there. Let's get the hell out of here."

Then, a different guy knocked hard and fast on the front door. Rose hugged herself tight and shook in fear.

With pinpoint focus she prayed so hard it hurt, *God, if you make them go away and never come back I promise I will find a safer place to live.*

A third voice, bored and restless, "Let's go."

> *Time to make a stand,*
> *Time to live for me,*
> *Time to open my mind,*
> *Time to see the truth.*

Not all who Wander are Lost
JRR Tolkien

Anti-Vietnam War demonstrations marched into the lives of everyone Rose knew. It was impossible to focus on her studies. In sociology class at Merritt Jr. College she met Jeff, a lanky, granny glasses wearing, nineteen year old guy. Addicted to weed and hallucinogens, Jeff possessed the ego-driven drive to lead others.

A thick mist rolled into Berkeley from San Francisco the afternoon that Rose and Jeff strolled to the college parking lot. Rose felt a dying need to share, "Last night three guys were hanging outside my place banging on the door talking trash. God knows what they would have done if they got in. I was scared shitless."

"Listen girl, I can tell you've got a heart of gold and the strength of a tiger. We could use some hot blooded women to fight those damn politicians. There's a room opening up at my place. Come by and check it out."

"When?"

"How about now."

"Sure."

"Follow me."

One of the many outspoken men challenging the government's leaders, he lived in a frat house that had been taken over by the "radicals." After more sweet convincing words Rose rented a room in the "Hearst Castle" on the corner of Hearst Avenue and La Loma Drive, dropped out of college, landed a job at a pizza parlor on Telegraph Avenue and became a protestor.

Rose didn't have an orthodox religious personality. She believed in the power of faith and the understanding that all people have a place on this earth with unique lessons to learn and valuable contributions to make to society. She felt that our complex civilization needs their differences. Nonetheless, she was a Quaker. They are pacifists. They believe in equality regardless of sex, race, or social position. Quakers partake in war efforts as only medics, doctors and nurses.

In 1969 and 1970, Rose belonged to an independent, spiritual, creative, rebellious willful group of men and women who heavily questioned the values their parents had set for them and the actual cause and purpose of the Vietnam War. They were not willing to go along with President Lyndon B. Johnson's forced draft.

On December 1, 1969, President Johnson implemented the "Lottery Drawing." Ping pong balls labeled with birthdates ready and waiting to be read out loud shot out of a tube. Fearful citizens of the United States of America waited for their friends', boyfriends', sons' birthdays' to be announced on TV or the radio. It would determine the future of their lives. Young men Rose knew or barely knew were "called up" to be sought out for a war they didn't want to fight. The 92nd date was called. It was her birthday. She would have had to go or face becoming a draft dodger and labeled a coward except for the fact that she was a woman. Her sex alone determined that she was ineligible for physical or psychological death. The shock of her destiny affected her profoundly. For years Rose had wished she were male. Jobs were easier to acquire and being independent wasn't as likely to be a social threat. The day her birth date was "called up," she felt more grateful to be female than she ever had in her life.

The internal war of choices began for Rose's male friends to find a way out: become a conscientious objector, open to beatings; face incarceration; leave the country (Canada, Mexico, Sweden, Norway or France); go to the draft physical on LSD; dress in drag; become emaciated or obese; maim themselves so badly that the military would not want them; have a legitimate physical deferment; present proof of your affiliation with a religion against barring arms; become fathers or stay in school. Even with the great efforts made by many men, the chances of it working were slim.

The Quaker Meeting House in Berkeley was open to all men in need. Counselors gave suggestions on how to fill out forms, giving them a chance to prove they were unfit for military service. Lies were the truth behind many a man's ability to dodge the draft. Men through out the United States found ways to live their own lives, not the life President Johnson thought they should.

It was a frightening time. They battled for their self-worth through a sea of regimented mania. Protesting against the Vietnam War was what they ate and breathed until the government stopped their hunger to control the people who weren't interested in fighting a battle that wasn't theirs to fight.

Rose supported those men who felt the force of the "Lottery Drawings" and had the emotional strength to revolt. Some men rebelled quietly, others overtly, but nonetheless stood by their personal need to be free of dictatorship.

While living in the "Heart Castle," Rose was driven into a world of intense rebellion against the power of conservative and dominant thought patterns. A variety of meetings took place in the dining room of the three story building designed for the privileged male students of the University of California Berkeley campus. Rose was one of five women among twenty young adults. They amassed and discussed the Vietnam War, Gay Rights, Women's Liberation and the rent strike, all the while smoking weed and experimenting in hallucinogenic drugs.

At the demonstrations on the University of California Berkeley campus, law enforcement officers in heavy gear and face masks shot tear gas into their eyes, assaulted them if they even slightly resisted an order. Being pushed pulled and hit by the "Pigs" was demoralizing. Down to her core, Rose reacted with anger and fear. For the weeks and months that she protested against the War she deeply identified with the young men in Vietnam that had absolutely no control over their lives because of a few cold-hearted, power-hungry men in leadership roles. The Vietnam War was their war. They needed bodies to do the dirty work and to look strong and protective. Countless young adults, including Rose, refused to be victims.

Rose's personality was far too sensitive to cope with the loss of mental stability that drugs and demonstrations brought with them. The turning point was instigated by a drug pusher living in the "Heart Castle." LSD laced with mescaline given in very small doses, could and did, keep a thin minimal user like her high for hours. She ingested a pill late one afternoon. An acute awareness of the thoughts and feelings of others and the goings on throughout the frat house crept through her like a vile disease. She stumbled outside, stepped into the street and was then mesmerized by a single beam of a car's headlights piercing into her eyes. The thought of allowing the oncoming traffic to end her life floated through her thoughts like a reassuring open door to a warm and safe cocoon. Without a moment to spare, Rose side-stepped onto the sidewalk and willed herself back to her room.

In the midst of Rose's involvement with political upheavals, calls to and from her family were rare and all too frequently shortened by Mother, "Can't talk long, costs too much."

After far too many "it costs too much" Rose began phoning. Unrelenting her family continued to remind her of the cost of a long distance call. She simply wanted to speak freely. As time went by her gesture was taken for granted and unappreciated. Regardless of their financial state, they were frugal to the point of ridiculous, filled with unrealistic fears. The rooms with no doors in their home protected them from outside influences. They had lived during the depression. Father was especially affected. Care as she did Rose took any and all opportunities to forget their world.

The hopelessness and fatigue of the never ending attempts to stop conservative thought and the actions of those in authority, but moreover Rose's drive to be something as an individual changed her focus back to the rural world. The anti-Vietnam War efforts continued without her.

At the end of 1970 her housemate comrade and lover Roman, was one of the many spokesmen for the Berkeley rent strikes and a participant in the Gay Rights parades. Along with his calico cat Miss Kitty, Rose and he left Berkeley in her 1968 VW Bug. They hung out with Rose's old classmate Jill, for a few weeks and then played house in the foothills of the Sierra Nevada Mountains. A charming curly long dark haired and mustache twenty-one years old cute guy, Rose adored him. He landed a dishwashing job at Denny's in Kindle City, egg-crated a room off of the kitchen, played his guitar to his heart's content and gave guitar lessons in his spare time. Rose joined the dance classes offered at Penelope's Dance Studio, cared for the dog and cat and took on the role of the homemaker, but it wasn't enough. Her childhood dream to be a professional dancer welled up in her heart.

Our town's roller rink was my parent's form of cheap babysitting. There, we had a ball. I made friends or met-up with school mates. Exhilarating mood music, strobe lights, a far reaching floor, hamburgers, hot dogs, popcorn and old worn-out rented red and white leather roller skates that always hurt when I first put them on, made up that world. I soon forgot any notion of pain as the freedom of gliding through and around the crowded roller rink filled my spirit. I could skate for hours. The only thing that ever stopped me was the dreaded "couples skate." Lucky for me, it didn't last long. Eventually the "all skate" was announced over the loud speaker. I would jump out of my seat, roll onto the oval hardwood floored rink once again through the maze of bodies, delighted and free.

Penelope recommended that Rose go to Davis to study modern dance as a drop-in at the University of California and investigate other possibilities within the city limits. After driving twice-a-week for six months to Davis, her aspirations to dance led to a conversation with Ms. Scott that changed her life. Direct, forthcoming and truly inspiring she said, "You will never find the caliber of dance classes you are looking for unless you move to the Bay Area. You have the heart and drive to be a dancer, but your instrument, your body, is not educated in the art of dance. You have a lot of work to do. Two very kind men from New York's professional dance community started a modern dance center in Berkeley about ten years ago. It could be what you're looking for. Good luck."

It was exactly what she needed.

But one month shy of Rose's twenty-first birthday, an emotional bomb fell into her lap that catapulted her even harder into the next phase of her life. Rose's stern, frustrated father and she hadn't seen or spoken to each other since his brief visit to Indiana. In response to a neighborhood gossip filled letter from Mother, she called her on a payphone at the local laundromat only a stone's throw from the little house Roman and Rose rented. She needed to let Mother know how happy she was in her new home.

Mother answered, "Hello," her tone a bit suspicious.

"Mother it's me, I'm so happy to be back in Kindle City. Roman and I..."

Father screamed, "Who is it?" his insistence to know anything that went on in his house persisting beyond reason.

Apprehensive, "Gilbert, it's Rose."

"Give me the phone this minute."

Rose's throat tightened at the very sound of his voice. Father knew she lived with a man whom he had not met. Mother met Roman during one of her flights of fancy to her daughter's world at "Hearst Castle." The two of them sucked weed together. Mother was curious and appeared interested in the lifestyle that her daughter had chosen, but it was the men that intrigued her the most. In her sixties obese and sedentary, Rose's mother still possessed alluring eyes.

"What's the big deal? It doesn't do a thing for me," detached, unaware of the fact that she sucked in very little.

Mother especially enjoyed flirting with Roman. In a private moment he complained to Rose, but she knew it wouldn't stop her. It was one of her mother's habits that she chose not to control around the men Rose cared for. It was an excellent opportunity for her to come between Rose and her happiness with a man.

But that day Father grabbed the receiver, screaming at the top of his lungs, "You're a good-for-nothing whore. Roman, if that's his real name, is using you. What's wrong with you? Have you lost your mind?"

Rose forced herself not to yell, but she had to be bold.

Disgusted and in disbelief that the father she once called Daddy could say such a thing, "I'm not that person you speak of. If I were, YOU are the one who turned me into her. You and Mother brought Luke into our home, not me!"

She could hear Mother in the background, "Gilbert, stop it. She won't come home if you keep talking to her like that."

It did not stop him.

Stunned and shaking, Rose hung up. In a daze she went home. Father's words echoed in her jarred psyche. She needed to explain the call to Roman, but how?

Roman was on her side, but that single conversation with her father put a wall between them no matter what he said. Rose knew who she was. She knew who Roman was, or did she? A seed of doubt was planted. It crept into their lives like a slow acting poison.

Within a week, she received a second letter from Mother. Father was in a car accident. Stanley was eighteen years old. What was he going to do without his father, if it came to that? Mother's letters had at numerous times clued her in to how attached Father and Stanley were.

Stanley, a six feet five inches, oversized head and lanky boy was always smiling. He stuffed his food into his mouth then let the juices drip down his chin. The droppings landed on his shirt. Without a care in the world, he drank a full can of soda at once then wiped his face with his bare arm or shirt sleeve. He appeared dumb to most people, didn't make eye contact except when something he read struck him. Then there was no stopping him. Information flew out of his mouth unfettered.

His classmates harassed him on the playground and to and from school, "retard, four-eyes, scarecrow," taunting him, not letting up unless someone, anyone, mostly me, stopped them.

He didn't respond. He trudged away, face to the ground.

I yelled, "Leave him alone, he's not doing anything to you," and then too embarrassed to say another word I also turned away and went on with my life without him. I hated myself, but I couldn't face the taunting boys' evil minds.

It was a heart attack. Father was speeding down the road in the family car. He ran a red light, was hit by the approaching vehicle and then rushed to the hospital.

Rose was deeply confused and wanted to understand what happened.

She called, "Can I help? Do you need me?"

Mother's response, "Your father gained quite a bit of weight since you last saw him. He's depressed. It wasn't the argument that the two of you had that caused his emotional outburst. It was much more. I can handle things," fed a deep-rooted wedge.

When my dad had a job and the day's work was done he parked his car in our garage and then walked through the mudroom that had been converted into the pantry and laundry room. I was always excited to see him when I was small. Hoping for a sugar treat, I ran to meet him. One afternoon he sped down the driveway, screeched to a halt, shoved his shoulder into the car door and slammed it shut and then with vehemence pulled the backdoor open. With a single swipe of his left hand he backhanded me. I flew into the cupboard. Mom or Dad never picked me up, hugged me or apologized. That one blow to my face permanently crooked my jaw. Only when I talked was it visible, but as a little girl I didn't talk much. Coldness and fear set into my heart and soul. From that day on, "Mom and Dad" became "Mother and Father."

For five days Mother sat at her husband's bedside in the hospital.

Mother wrote, "Your father died of cardiac arrest. There will be no memorial. His papers are in order. I'll send the monies you are entitled to. He did think of you."

Rose was ready to be free of her family, but that last conversation with her father oozed its way into her self-esteem. Unanswered questions took hold. His opinion mattered. He was an old man with little purpose, but he was still her daddy. She wouldn't hear his voice telling her of the mice family way up in the sky or feel his comforting bulk as she did when she was four.

Mom and Dad turned on the family's phonograph player or Dad would get out his violin and Mom would accompany him on the piano. It was soothing to my soft heart to look and listen to them create an atmosphere that they loved. Sometimes, Dad would put down his violin and ask me to dance while a favorite tune filled the living room.

Dad's eyes sparkled, "You're my little girl, come dance with me," opening the palms of his huge hands softly pulling me to an embrace.

I stood on his feet as he danced a perfect waltz. His hands, big and rough held my little ones in front of him. My head barely reached his knees. To finish a delightful musical evening, Dad dropped to his knees and began to sing to me with dramatic flourish, adornment and pride. I believed every word as he sang one of his favorite songs, "I Believe."

I believe with every drop of rain that falls a flower grows.

I believe that somewhere in the darkest night a candle glows.

I believe for everyone who goes astray someone will come to show the way.

I believe, I believe.
I believe above the storm the smallest prayer will still be heard.
I believe that someone in the great somewhere hears every word.
Every time I hear a new-born baby cry, or touch a leaf, or see the sky, then I know why I believe.

Lyrics and music

Erin Drake   Erin Graham   Jimmy Shirl   Al Stillman

The news of Father's death shifted Rose's entire world to possibilities. Before that day her dreams were put in the category of the unspeakable. Today, there was one less person to look to for permission to be her.

The hardship that crushed her as a child fed Rose's ambition. Her needs extended beyond Father's authority. She had no trepidations about the life she was about to make for herself. It was going to be a new, exciting life far beyond her dark, troubled upbringing. She had to be herself. She had to put his opinion of her into the abyss of her mind or go insane.

With a picture in hand of actor, feminist and political strategist, Jane Fonda, Rose got a haircut.

"A woman who cuts her hair is about to change her life."
Co Co Chanel

Part Three

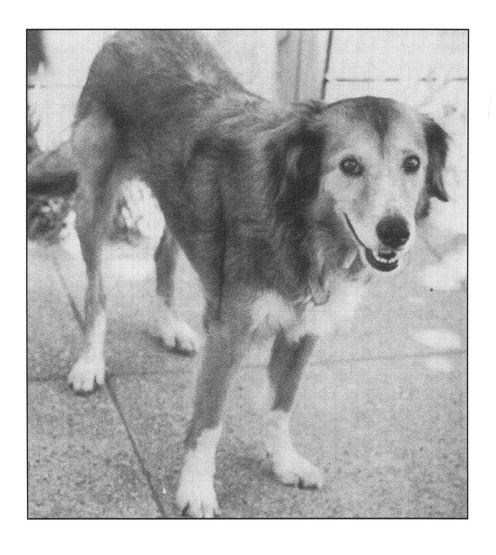

*"It is very peaceful to be able to live for your work alone.
The self-denial, the sacrifices that our work demands are all
compensated for by that lovely serenity of giving
yourself up to dance."*
Edward Villela

It was April of 1971. Rose was twenty-one years old and full to the brim with determination and focus. A one year old Border Collie-Saluki named Brandi, accompanied her in her VW Bug in search of the Shawl-Anderson Modern Dance Center in Berkeley.

The moment Rose stepped into the center she was awed at the very sight of the professional dancers milling about in the lobby and of the pictures on the walls of those who came before them. With hope and a fierce desire to learn, she handed the clerk a check for a month worth of classes, five days a week, one class a day.

"Are you sure? This is a lot of money and you have never been here before."

Trying so hard not to pierce into the eyes of the curious and protective clerk Rose vocalized her long awaited wish polite and real, "Yes, very sure. This school was highly recommended. I need to do this," moisture welling up in her eyes.

She floated out the door, buckets and buckets of tears streaming down her cheeks.

The vagueness of her life had ended. She was no longer lost in a pool of fantasies. She had money in the bank and knew how to live simply and wouldn't live outside her means.

At 9:45 in the morning, Rose pulled open the heavy stained glassed oriental door, maneuvered through the narrow gap that she had allowed herself and then proceeded to the receptionist's desk. Without a word she signed the role sheet, headed for the dressing room and then climbed the two flights of stairs to her first professional modern dance class.

Clothed in a leotard and tights a barefooted Rose began the process of learning to be a precise mover among ten other modern dance students. Ceiling to floor mirrors surrounded the empty hardwood floored dance studio.

Rose's first professional dance teacher, Victor Anderson was a soft spoken, direct man who stood straight and tall and moved with grace. Rose could feel the respect he had for himself. He made designs and movements with an ease completely foreign to anything she had ever seen that close.

The image in the mirror of her attempts to repeat his moves immediately caused alarm. Rose's ability to correct herself was reachable, but unseasoned. After a correction, self-imposed or otherwise, she was embarrassed. Rose wanted to run out the center's front door. But driven to learn and Victor Anderson's empathy toward beginners, like her, his sincere words of encouragement and small constructive criticism kept her in the room.

The next day she met Frank Shawl. He was a curly-haired outgoing man, his smile stretched to the walls of any room in which he inhabited. At the beginning of his modern dance class, when the mood of the classroom was glum, he'd say with the knowing of one who has been there, "All the responsibilities and problems you have outside of this room will still be there after you are gone. For now, for the next hour-and-a-half, leave them at the door and allow yourself to be embraced by the movement, music and essence of dance." Those words pulled Rose up and gave her life meaning.

The following morning Rose took Luisa Pierce's class. Luisa, the first teacher to be hired by the Shawl-Anderson Modern Dance Center possessed an extensive repertoire. To her, all movement had to mean something. She shot from her gut Martha Graham's technique coupled with the Lester Horton's isolated shoulder-elbow-or-hip originated off balance-to-balance technique. Luisa was dynamic, electric and passionate in all that she expressed as a teacher.

Rose was taken aback. Was there even a remote chance that she could do what Luisa wanted from her? Rose didn't have to explain herself to Luisa, but she had to show the depth of her feelings through movement. Words didn't come easy for Rose, but she loved to move. Consequently, as frightened as she was of Luisa's approach to modern dance, in time, Rose accepted and then came to appreciate Luisa's approach to dance as a means to remove herself from her shell safely.

Within the first year of studying professional modern dance and practicing on her own in any space inside or out that gave her room to move her body strengthened as well as her resolve.

It was long after her days as a ballerina with the San Francisco Ballet when Evelyn C. Schuert glided into Rose's life. Evelyn was in her fifty's. Rose was twenty-two. This was Rose's chance to be taken in by a "jewel of a teacher."

Evelyn was glamorous, intuitive and highly educated in the art of ballet. She drifted into the center dressed in black from head to toe. Her hair deep velvet black tied back in a bun. She wore a long cape and skirt that rippled when she proceeded to the dressing-room in her sensible shoes. A touch of make-up added to her stately entrance into the center. She removed her cape and shoes to reveal a black scoop-neck long sleeved leotard and donned her black ballet slippers.

Evelyn's ballet barre, the talk of the Bay Area, was said to be one of the most difficult among the top-notch professional dancers. Her choice of words was pleasant, but firm. When Rose needed her gentle support, with great discretion Evelyn's touch alone put her body into the correct line.

With four dance teachers leading the way, Rose took on the long-term challenge of making her body an instrument of creation. Every waking hour she lived and breathed dance. Day after day, month after month, that led into years, she stood in front of her mentors watching, zeroing in on every gesture, movement and words of advice. She had to see and then feel what she saw. The repetitive practice was painstaking, difficult and frustrating. Rose's self-image, persistence and eye-body awareness was constantly challenged.

Fulfilling Rose's primary goal to move, feel and express in the classroom or on stage what was in her heart and soul drove her on when the dripping sweat, fatigue, aches, floor burns, calloused feet, ego deflating or building became an ongoing reality.

Rose's determination, focus and dedication shined through. Her mentors noticed her intent, the seriousness of her desires and consequently shared their extensive experience in the art of dance.

Beyond anything Rose believed possible, her body developed the muscles that were needed to become a proficient mover. Gifted with a feel for music, her response to rhythm and sound came from a place deep within and permeated every motion she made. Her mind was linked to her body placement, the line and flow of the movements and the rhythm of the counts, drums or piano. Gestures flowed one into another and then another, shape after shape, movement into movement allowing her the opportunity to control the passage of her body and emotions through space.

As the world of dance opened up to Rose she discovered a place to belong and comrades within the wordless language of movement. Enveloped within the reflection of ceiling to floor mirrors their energy was with one another, the music and the inspiring words of their mentors. At the same time, as individuals, they had to connect with their center of balance, tell their feet, legs and torsos to spring them from the wooden floor to another shape and then become the movement. The fellowship gave Rose a sense of wholeness, belonging and freedom.

"The universe is presenting you with an opportunity to take courage and soar above the mundane of your life."
                                        David Carson

I couldn't break my sense of being at fault for the dysfunction that showed up in my life down to its components.

The Shawl-Anderson Modern Dance Center was the lighthouse in the sea of the unknown. The hour and a half dance classes gave Rose the opportunity to focus her mind and body on the teachings of dance. Nonetheless, her need to make money and provide shelter to not only herself, but her dog Brandi, was paramount.

Periodically, requests forms for work to be done at the center in exchange for free or discounted classes showed up on the receptionist desk next to the role sheet. Upon Rose's arrival in Berkeley, she plunged into the money Mother gave her when she left to go east. It was imperative that she lower her costs. Thrilled to get the opportunity to be a stronger part of the center, she signed up to clean the dance studio and to document the signatures from the roll-sheet into the center's ledger.

For months, she had pined for stability. Now, she felt appreciated and at ease within the compounds of the center. Its phone number was the one to find her. Open to the public 9am to 10pm, the center was always there.

Rose's late nights and early mornings were in flux. After skimming the center's and college campus bulletin boards she rented single rooms in places she could afford. For five years, defenseless against the whims of others she and Brandi slept in cold leaky attics, dismal basements or loud door-less dining rooms with bathrooms down the hall. She stuffed single bags of groceries in run-down refrigerators and slipped her dry goods into designated shelves in communal kitchens that weren't always there when she was hungry. The rooms were all temporary, her suitcase and Brandi's bowl close-at-hand.

A nomad in the face of lodging the center gave her the security that kept Rose's life and dream afloat.

But beyond the safe and nurturing walls of her dance world it was impossible not to dip into the teasing pools of desire. Beautiful, single, strong and agile men walked the streets of Berkeley and Oakland. Not ending until 1975, the Vietnam War pulled the heterosexual men away from their hopes and dreams when they were just beginning to germinate. The black and white couples no longer hid. Men and women scrutinized their lives more profoundly than the generation before considered possible. Some believed the same sex was a more exciting and satisfying connection. Getting high to mute the pain, frustrations and realities of the war was rampant. It led men and women to distance themselves from any kind of stable relationship.

A physical beauty, an independent streak and will-power coupled with the notion of love deep and enduring put Rose in a dynamic flip-flop of morals. Emotional stability was difficult, verging on impossible, but she held hope for a man in her life.

A majority of women, including her, faced the social pressure and quest for the freedom to have sex without the fear of pregnancy. Taking birth control pills, using diaphragms or practicing the rhythm method were the norm. Health care practitioners were deeply concerned with the possibilities of unwanted pregnancies, venereal diseases and the AID's virus was accelerating in the Bay Area.

Without fail, the health care practitioners asked, "Are you sexually active?" as a part of a female exam.

"Yes," was, without a doubt, Rose's answer, truth or not.

She was caught up in the simple lie of a man in her life to gain access to a prescription of her chosen form of birth-control.

After a short lecture addressing self-respect, unwanted pregnancies and a handful of pamphlets describing the various form of venereal diseases she was let go, well-supplied with contraceptives.

The need to fit in held a grip on Rose's underlying low self-esteem. Wanting the affections of men she lost her individuality within the loose environment. She set aside the moral ethics that she cultivated to free herself from her family. Needing boundaries, but no power to build them, the paradox led her to an inner conflict that only solitude could alleviate. But Rose loved to go to parties and dance.

College students, professors and professionals of all walks of life gathered at the parties. They were full of gay and straight men and women. How to tell them apart was a skill Rose slowly acquired. It was in the eyes and their way of moving, but mostly it was who they gravitated towards and how they touched each other.

At first Rose watched in horror, but she realized that homosexual men wouldn't under any circumstances want her to perform the violent act of sex that she couldn't forget. They were safe.

Lovely gay men spent a great deal of time primping. Aggressive and above board short haired women wore baggy jeans and plaid flannel shirts. They stood out far more than the long flowing haired and cotton floral dressed feminine women that "came on" to her. Stunned, she politely refused and then edged her way through the crowd.

At the parties and on the "Pill", Rose fully acknowledged her intentions of getting laid. She had a bit to drink, danced with a testosterone driven man to then follow him to a corner or an empty bedroom and have sex. She went home with hers or his phone number in a pocket.

When Rose and a man connected for the night her forced undercover personality of the distant past surfaced and allowed her to do things with a man completely foreign to her current persona. Under the disillusions of love Rose performed the sexual acts that he desired. Unknowingly capable of destroying her, his wishes were fulfilled. The nights in bed with Luke, the caressing between her and Michael and then Alex drifted into her spirit. It was what she knew she could be for a man. The function was available in a heartbeat.

Day and weeks went by with no phone call. It broke her thin glassed heart.

The men that took interest, lengthy passionate interest, Rose tried to be what she thought they wanted her to be. Unbeknownst to her they were playing her.

With lighting speed the curtain of falsehood opened up, the question of survival pulled her independent spirit to the forefront. Rose ran.

But Albert wouldn't let go. He called and called long after Rose cut him off. Screaming, "Bitch, where the hell have you been? What's wrong with you? I want you and I want you now."

Unable to speak and her hands shaking in fear, Rose set down the receiver quietly, ever so quietly.

Albert was a bold and beautiful black man. He lived on the street Rose rode her bike to and from her basement room and the center. He had called her over one day to ask directions. So taken by his good looks and attentiveness Rose allowed herself to be lured into his duplex, have a drink, talk a bit, have sex and then become his property.

It took Rose to places long ago learned to rid Albert from her life. The skill of avoidance and polite reserve if only and only if their paths crossed was her ally. Late one evening, long after Rose thought he was out of her life, Albert had the telephone operator interrupt her phone conversation with her ex-lover turned friend Roman. He had joined her in her love of dance.

She reluctantly accepted the call.

His driving arrogant demand, "Where the hell have you been? I need to see you," brought fear into the depth of her being.

Rose pulled herself together and then in even tones revealed a newly formed self-regard, "I can't see you. Stop calling me. It's not going to work, you and me. I'm too busy."

Proud and stern he declared, "OK, bitch," and slammed the receiver down into its cradle.

Rose took a deep breath to fill her fear filled emptied lungs and then clasped her face with her hands.

Roman called back. Covered by a shaky laugh he stammered, "Be careful...Make yourself scarce...I love you."

Ever so grateful to have a guy in her life that knew her, she softly responded, "I will. Thanks ever so much. I love you too. I need to get to bed. Bye for now."

Fondly, Roman said, "Bye sweetie."

If Rose loved herself she would have never gone beyond the first hello, much less, allowed a penis-driven man to penetrate her body and soft heart.

With absolutely no desire to wait and wonder if a man was going to ask her to dance, she drank gin and tonic on an empty stomach and then danced to the music she loved. In the wee hours of the morning, Rose drove home after eating enough to mute the "buzz."

To be available to the performing dance community was Rose's life. She went back to dance, always dance, to find solidarity. That's what she wanted and that's how she found herself. If not, Rose would completely lose any perspective of personal value.

Encouragement is one of the great powers over man.
R.L. Wing

Luisa Pierce needed two teacher's assistants in exchange for unlimited classes at the center. Rose was a vital twenty-three years old, tall slim elongated muscled and limber sensuous woman. Her dance abilities were blooming. When Luisa approached Rose with her needs, it was a profound pleasure to accept the position. Luisa was never one to mince words or relinquish her place in the world of dance. Rose feared not being capable of demonstrating for her, but there was enough, in fact, plenty of reasons for her to believe in herself. Hours and hours of learning her technique had long past.

Luisa belted out the parts of the body that must be engaged to fulfill the combination. Rose was now in front of the class. All eyes were on her. It was Rose's very first performance. The attention, the pressure to be in the presence of a great dancer and do what she had done was powerful. Rose watched her image in the mirror with intent. Her strength to assist one who she admired filled Rose's spirit with a self-regard unknown to her until that day. It was unnerving, but she couldn't let on. People were counting on her. She was counting on herself.

Love as she did to be there for the center's needs, Rose's needs were mounting. She approached an ambitious businesswoman and student of dance in the process of establishing her Capezio Dance Theatre Shop in the East Bay and landed a part-time job. All the cashier and public relationship skills she had fed the new job requirements.

Rose clothed customers in dancewear and made informed suggestions in the application of theatre make-up. She learned to fit ballet slippers and pointe shoes as well as how to screw taps in-place on tap shoes. Feet are as unique as the personalities that they carry. Rose's sensitivity to touch assisted her. Touching a person's foot, like any other part of the body, must be done with care.

She learned how the human foot, when asked to move through space, must have the correct fitting shoe or the balance and mobility need to be a precise mover is affected. Although going on pointe was never a priority to Rose, she respected and appreciated those who did.

All walks of the dance-theater life arrived at the shop. It opened her heart to the multitude of life styles that populated the Bay Area.

Rose was a perfectionist in her work. She knew the stock inside and out. Try as she did to not create competition or jealousy it was unavoidable. The owner and the other employees found it difficult to appreciate her. Her one weakness or as she preferred to see it her strength, her individuality separated her from the shops clan. Although she had a flare for design and color she was never asked to decorate the windows or walls of the shop. Those who were in favor with the owner had that right.

It was an atmosphere Rose didn't want to prescribe to, nor did she know how to alleviate it. She wanted to do the best job she could that was all. She wanted to get along and at the same time be the strong person she was. But there was always that competitive edge to cause conflict. To her she was competing with herself not them, but it was fruitless to believe that they could ever share her way.

One year later, Rose's next job came about when, Mike, a fellow dancer and member of two well-established art-modeling agencies proposed the idea that she be an artist's model. He was a good man, a kind man, a man who wouldn't harm her. She trusted him. Being nude in front of people was familiar to her, but not until after a long conversation with Mike that described the job and much deliberation did she chose the self-employed position of an art model.

Rose was required to arrive on time in her personal vehicle, do the work and then collect her wage at the end of each session. The cost of gas for the long miles to and from each job was covered by the artist that had requested her skills. Ten percent of her earnings went to the booking agent. She believed this to be a logical and respectful way to do business.

The life drawing classes were taught in the Bay Area's colleges. Struggling dedicated art-students and professional artists also organized small group gatherings in their studio or home to develop their skills.

Rose was ecstatic to have the opportunity to invent a style. Many a three-hour class consisted of at least thirty model created poses. These poses were held for anywhere from thirty seconds to twenty minutes with a five-minute break every twenty minutes.

The agency had ethical rules to protect her. Only one time Rose felt the need to complain of the conduct of an employer.

Allen, the booking agent, took immediate action. He called the one in question and then declared, "No one is allowed the use of a model if the rules are broken. We are professionals. No one touches or expresses lewd behavior in the presence of the model during his or her working hours. In the future, don't call unless you intend to abide by the rules."

Rose was never asked to work for him again. Consolation rushed through her being. Allen was the first male in her life to defend her in such a way.

Allen treated the models as if they were his bosses and acknowledged how much he depended on them. Rose carried a mutual respect for him and never failed to have his ten percent fee stored away.

For all that I did to escape my childhood, like a plant not completely pulled out by its roots it grows back.

After her father's death, her visits to the family home were short and uncommon, but more than when he was alive. Now just the two of them, Mother and Stanley were on their own in the house Rose grew up in. The structure was unchanged. It was their lost world, lost in time. The walls were marked by scratches and holes left unfixed from fights between Art and Father long ago. They hadn't been painted since Father was alive. Now yellowed and blackened with grease and grime. Mimi's lovely antique furniture that Mother had inherited was hidden under piles and piles of unwashed dishes, books and magazines.

She treaded lightly into the unkempt front room and said with love in her heart, "How have you been? It's been a while."

Without fail, Mother and Stanley briefly glanced her way. Mother annoyed and short said, "The house could use a going over."

"Yes, but how are you?"

Repeating one after the other, "We don't see it, as you very well know," and then going right back to their reading material in the mist of clutter and filth.

Rose was aware, but didn't want to accept that her grandmother, Mimi, didn't believe anyone could perform household tasks at the high level to which she was accustomed. Consequently, she never took the time to teach her only child household chores beyond the feminine matched role of ironing and drying dishes. Father took on the role of homemaker. Although he insisted that Mother does the laundry.

When I was tall and strong enough, Mother and I did the laundry. It was our time together. I felt needed. I had a purpose in her life.

Every week, a few times a week we'd separate the clothes, dark or light. Then after they were washed clean we'd hang them out to dry. The wooden clothespins were held inside a canvas clothespin bag that hung from the back door handle right at my shoulder level. The basket of wet clothes sat on the upper step to the backyard and garage ready to be handed, by me, to Mother, one at a time. Then Mother pinned the clothes to the revolving multi-lined clothesline that was right outside the back door. She had a systematic approach. Each garment was connected to the next. There was no room for overuse of a clothespin or space. Father's and my brother's pants were provided with spring loaded pant stretchers. Mother did all the ironing and she was not about to iron any more than necessary.

It was Mimi who taught a young Rose how to clean, cook and be ladylike. She had become Mimi's shadow. Mother would have nothing to do with it.

The assumption that Rose was to take on the position of the chief cook and bottle washer whenever she visited annoyed her to no end. Nonetheless, for many a visit she complied. It filled a need, the need to do for her family, but it was eating her up.

Days before a visit, protected by the distance and detachment of the phone, Rose stated with a firmness unknown to Mother and Stanley, "This visit and all other visits in the future are not to be spent cleaning. I am coming to visit you, not clean your house. I'm not your maid."

Rose stumbled into their cramped living room. She stood over and waited while staring at a chair piled with newspapers. A six foot four inches tall, Stanley shoved them off. Not accustomed to his defiance, Rose cringed taken aback by a person who once followed her like a puppy.

Embedded in her caved-in lounge chair, wordless and arrogant Mother gawked at Rose for arduous seconds, "The bathroom tub, sink and floor need scrubbing. We left it for you. You always do such a good job."

"No," Rose declared.

Mother responded, "Why?" completely disregarding what she knew to be true.

About to weaken, Rose took an extensive, buried in the bowels of the earth, breath, looked at her mother in wonder to then say, "I called and told you why."

In time, a time that felt like hours, Mother's brow furrowed. She barely looking up from her book when she responded, "We didn't think you meant it."

Rose lifted her back straight and tall and then stated, "I did. I did mean it."

Shrugging her shoulders and kneading her hands together in a tight knot on her lap Mother declared, "We'll see."

An anger long left behind came to the surface, "Mother, you'll see. I've had it. Clean your own damn house."

Mother and Stanley went back to their books. Rose stepped outside and then sat down on the cement walkway that led to the sidewalk and glanced up and down the street of her lost innocence.

Needing to relieve herself she made her way back into the house. All the while thinking, "Damn it, there's nowhere else to go." She minced over left-to-rot and heavy-with-dust objects to then wedge herself to the bathroom. Now accustomed to using doors and locks she insisted on closing the door. The door was jammed up against the wall. She removed piles of magazines, newspapers that were leaning up against the doorjambs. And then she shoved a table that held their collection of telephone books away from in front of the bathroom door.

"What are you doing?" They shouted from opposite ends of the house.

"Mother, I'm closing the door."

Stanley's statement, "We never do that," was hard to take, but it was them, their life not hers.

Mother's support, "Leave her alone," carried them past a potentially explosive argument.

Stanley was in his mid twenties, a strong, tall, very tall, opinioned man by then.

The door swung closed. Rose noted with awe as she pulled the crystal glass octagon door knob. It glistened beneath her fingers.

The blackened with grime greasy hardware opposed the elegance of the knob. Rose shivered at the sight of a solid brass sliding bolt. She fingered and then turned a feather-light slip-lock.

For two nights, Rose slept in her, now storage room-bedroom on the old creaky twin bed and used the bathroom lock with no comment from Mother, but Stanley stood outside the door waiting and knocking on the door until she was done. He pushed his way inside through the opened door to see if she had changed or "stolen" anything.

During a visit months later, Rose needed the use of the bathroom once again, but in shock she found herself having to announce, "The lock has been removed."

Mother's cold and all too familiar detached voice responded, "I didn't notice."

When Stanley stomped past the unlocked shut door Rose yelled, "Don't you dare open that door."

Stanley wined, "Mother, Rose is closing the door again."

"Leave her alone. She needs her privacy," was all she got from Mother.

Every visit thereafter, Mother said, "We need you here. You were such a good influence on Stanley and I can't keep house the way you do."

At that time, Rose's dance career hadn't quite jelled and the dance community in her family's neighborhood was growing. She considered moving back. Things were getting out of hand.

When Father was alive he had a room with an attached mini bathroom built behind the garage for guests, but mostly it was his writing studio. Rose thought how about if she were to move back home and in exchange for rent. She could keep the house in order and have some heart-to-hearts with Stanley. But it was only going to work if she had her own key to the room behind the garage. It had to be different than the house key and not in the possession of Mother or Stanley, especially Stanley. A space to park her car that was always available to her must be part of the deal. To her it was reasonable, objective and doable.

They went into hysterics, "You must live in the house and in your room, period. We want to know what you're up to."

Rose couldn't believe her ears. She stayed in Berkeley, stuck to her guns and never cleaned for them again.

Over the phone she made plenty of suggestions. But they were untaken.

It wasn't the money. They had plenty. Plenty to horde, to feel secure, untouched by the neighbors that lived only feet away from their house.

The idea, moreover the thought of someone else coming into their home to clean frightened Mother and Stanley to the point of an onset of a panic attack. "They might steal something. Talk about us. What will they think?"

Visits and phone calls went by in a daze, except the one when Mother told Rose that Luke had been in communication with her and Stanley for sometime. The worst of it was that Luke asked about her and wanted to see what she was up to.

Completely taken-off-guard and flabbergasted she said, "You must be kidding."

Mother insisted, "No, he really cares for you."

The shakes, nervous twitches and sweats plunged into Rose's essence. With pinpoint clarity she shouted out, "He doesn't know and never did know who I am. The answer is no and will always be no. I think you've lost your mind. To be associating with him at all is nuts. Mother, what does he have over you?"

Mother acknowledged Rose with a "hum" then void of any emotion whatsoever said, "OK I'll tell him, but can I at least give him your address and phone number so he can write or call."

Not answering the most important question. What he obviously has over her, sex.

"Mother that's insane, no."

"OK, dear, but..."

"But nothing, don't you dare give him my address or phone number, period."

If I had a gun, knew how to use it and wasn't a Quaker I would have killed him. But I didn't and I was.

Why they wanted to have anything to do with that evil man was impossible for Rose to understand. It was so clear how little they knew her, respected her and most important shared her life.

It was painfully odd for Rose to acknowledge the truth. On visits when she escaped the house to get air and exercise she heard tales from the neighbors of her life in the Bay Area. Mother boasted of Rose's career. The one she never took the time to see.

Rose saw and felt those terrible things and lived another day.

One's roots determine much of a life lived.

We can all be replaced, but no one can be copied.

In her forties, Luisa Pierce was diagnosed with breast cancer. Rose witnessed her seemingly endless passion and enduring commitment for dance-theatre subside as she succumbed to the chemo treatments. Unable to demonstrate the dance she loved.

With a heavy heart, Rose replaced Luisa's body in dance. A compliment laced in responsibilities, loss and the need for strength that Rose was unsure she could match.

As Luisa's dear friend, Victor Anderson had choreographed and then performed a duet with her titled "Auf Mir", a theatre piece based on the poem "Narcissus and Echo" by Fred Chappell, music by Cara Bradbury Marcus. Victor asked Rose to dance Luisa's part and Ian Cousineau, a fellow Shawl-Anderson Dance Company member, to replace himself. They were honored.

Rose played the part of Echo; Ian was Narcissus. Echo longed for Narcissus, but his attention was fixed on the only prop on stage, a full length wooden standing mirror frame. Narcissus couldn't take his eyes off of the imaginary reflection of himself intent on gazing and stretching his arm and extended fingers toward the oval beyond mere moments in time. Echo's futile attempts to lure, touch or speak to him maddened her. She laid her body down to no avail. To retreat was all she had to hold on to her tenuous self-esteem.

As with all the dances Rose was a part of, she did her best to fulfill the choreographer's wishes. Rose wasn't Echo, but she possessed an intense unfulfilled desire toward the opposite sex not altogether different from her.

Victor, a man of few words shared, "Rose, you danced beautifully," with a fondness for the movement arts and her, only found when two like-minded people meet.

Luisa never said a word. Rose was hurt. She wanted to say something, hug her and make it all go away, but Victor's looks when they shared a room said, "Let it go."

All that Luisa was for Rose was inside, very deep inside. Luisa gave her a safe place to open up. Rose had to believe she knew.

Rose continued to be her assistant until Luisa's strength waned to the point that no one beyond her intimate family and friends saw her. Her passing left a hole in the Shawl-Anderson Modern Dance Center.

One late morning, after studying ballet and modern dance for nine years, Rose was going down the stairs from the studio after her daily class. She was on her way to the dressing room.

Dripping and soaked in sweat, drained from the mental and physical exertion after Evelyn's ballet class Rose heard Victor's voice, "Do you have a minute?"

Taken aback by his allusive tone she responded, "Yes, of course. How have you been?"

"Just fine Rose. Evelyn and I have been talking about you lately and we would like you to know how much you have improved. We see your dedication and enjoy watching your progress. You have the heart and discipline to succeed."

A gift beyond explanation, Rose looked into his wet eyes and said in a whisper, "Thank you. It means a lot coming from the two of you."

Months later, following another of Evelyn's grueling classes, Rose and she shared their belief in the divine science of Astrology. Evelyn's interest in Rose's natal chart was a balm to her self-esteem. Astrology was Rose's beacon into her understanding of herself and the human condition.

A sincere concern for Rose's welfare came across when Evelyn spoke from her heart, "Rose, you have the grace and discipline to study ballet with the intensity of a professional ballerina, but your age, your body type, moreover your sensitivity will get the better of you in the competitive world. Ballet gives you such pleasure. Don't stop, but accept your limitations."

Rose was fully aware of how Evelyn kept her going when the cloud of discouragement descended. Ballet is a beautiful dance form. The precision is daunting, exhausting and beyond reach for some. In spite of it all, with teachers like Evelyn C. Schuert all your dreams can come true.

During Rose's final years as a performing modern dancer she yearned to expand beyond the safe walls of the center. A nightmare brought out the evil ways of street life in New York City. It put a halt to any hopes of challenging herself in the intense professional dance community of that city, but the Bay Area still had more to offer her.

She became a student of Marcia Sakamoto a small, determined woman who believed in the need to do a movement over and over again until the combination was embedded within the kinetic memory of the dancer's body. She detested mirrors and wouldn't allow them in her studio.

Rose had come from years of multi-mirrored classrooms and was overly conscious of her own image. Marcia offered her an opportunity to cut the cord and discover her body awareness free of the judgment of the mirrors. It was disconcerting when her addiction to the mirror was severed. Nonetheless, Rose welcomed the chance to go within.

For two years, Rose was a member of Marcia's dance company, Moving Space. She was in a quartet. It was satisfying, but she needed more. She could do more.

One day Marcia peeked into the dressing room, waved Rose to come near and then asked her to stay after class.

The dance studio emptied except for her and Marcia. She said, "Rose you need to be more mindful of your breath in relationship to movement, watch."

She filled her lungs to their capacity. Effortlessly, her body lifted to the balls of her feet. Then she forced her breath out, her chest curved inward, her arms and soft hands floated to the level of her waist. Her weight went backwards. She was on her heals about to fall, but quickly she caught herself by putting one foot behind her.

There was simplicity to Marcia's demonstration that made sense to Rose. On her own, she spent time simply moving with breath without the pressure of a choreographer's or teacher's direction or judgment. Consequently, Rose's experience as a performer coupled with Marcia's choreography created a dance titled "Breath Spirit," a silent solo.

Rose's breath alone served as the origin of movement. The costume, virtually invisible, created an eerie mystical figure under a single overhead fogged light. Rose's rhythmic breath and a full house at a seven hundred seating Auditorium in San Francisco marked a point in her identity that was ready to give birth, the birth of a soloist.

Being on my own was as familiar as the skin I wore.

"You are unique and if that is not fulfilled then something has been lost."
Martha Grahman

Rose's statue and social status had gradually unfolded beyond her wildest dreams. She was a skilled mover and a part of the dance world. Nonetheless, she never lost sight of the truth. Her grit and passion for dance gave her the respect of her mentors and comrades.

Aspiring as well as seasoned choreographers took notice. Rose was given opportunities to dance in an array of concerts. She took them without question. She wanted to learn and learn she did. They all contributed to her knowledge of the performing arts. Never a cent was passed on to her. The understanding and process of choreographing and then the teaching of a well designed performable piece was the gift.

It was a wish, a longing for Rose, getting to know her partner or the ensemble as people. It added a great deal of ease during the final dress rehearsal and performance. It softened her fear.

Painfully aware of the audience, Rose suffered from, if not honored, debilitating stage freight. To go beyond it, days and weeks of rehearsals went on before she was to the point of safety. She immersed herself in the dances so completely that she was virtually unaware of the audience. Every second of every moment of the dances were embedded in the cells of her body.

When the time came to rely on her kinetic memory she let go of the security of the mirrors that surrounded her in the studio. She acquainted herself with each stage, its problems and assets or she felt lost in the unfamiliar and possibility venerable to injury space. Backstage, dressing room, curtains and the floor, the position of the audience, lighting and then she noted spots beyond the stage that kept her in balance and helped her to recognize her position in relationship to the space.

Then it was time for the lights and sound to cue Rose to move. Centered and surrounded with an energy field for protection. She flew through space. She wouldn't allow herself to disappoint herself or her dance family. Nonetheless, she was aware of the points of light and dark holes in the audience where her friends and foe sat in judgment.

Nine years of ballet, and additional modern dance techniques that included Merc Cunningham, Jose Limon, Mime and Jazz under Rose's belt her movement vocabulary was extensive. She'd received recognition as "one of the better modern dancers in the Bay Area." As an artist's model Rose stored up poses that could, with her feel for continuity, be tied together to create a dance. She was twenty-nine years old and had sustained back and hamstring injuries. With work before class or a concert she continued to perform to the caliber that she had set her sights on years before.

Rose loved who she was and what she could do with her body. She needed to become all that she could be in the dance world. A world that belonged to the young, vibrant and dedicated, was about to end for her.

She combined choreographing three solos with the creation of new poses within the framework of the art classes.

There are some dances we're meant to do alone. "Darkness of Enclosed Space" expressed stagnate inner torment that longed to be released. The liquid, mystical and hypnotic "Rainbow Dome" music of Steven Hilage filled the stage.

A snowflake spotlight singled out the presence of a lone figure. Rose's short silky auburn hair, pitch black torso and thighs, an X on her back marked her place in life. Her facial expression was of fear, need and longing. Her forearms, calves and feet were raw, exposed to the elements.

Beginning in an angular sucked inside upright embryo shape upstage right Rose began the arduous task of releasing herself from bondage. Bound to the floor, a soft amber spotlight followed her in slow motion. A delicate easy touch and the broad extended flow of her legs propelled her down the diagonal line to stage left. Briefly, when the question of the beyond released her she stood knees bent absorbing the waterfall of her imagination. But the fear of the eyes of others floated into her soul. She collapsed to the floor. Crawling in deliberate tactile spider-like steps she crept forward. Her essence softening, Rose opened up and then allowed the circular flow of water surrounding and moving inside to calm her. To bring the piece to a close, she looked to the sky in hopes of discovering a future beyond the limitations of her mind.

To express the silly side of Rose, she created "Good Times," a bright and light expression of life's joy. A recording of Johnny Hodges' modern jazz of the 40s accompanied her. The music of the times long ago added to the euphoric atmosphere, as did a brown felt fedora that perched on Rose's head. A rainbow striped bow-neck cropped shirt, white billowy pants and a touch of sequins wrapped around her left ankle glistened as the carefree character pantomimed her way throughout the stage with fun-filled clown-like gestures. The ending combination, a delight, had a likeness to Charlie Chaplin's choreography.

In completion, Rose put together a dance portraying a woman in the process of blooming. "Cosmic Flower," Music by Jean Michel Jarre, a rippling coral dress gave a feminine touch to the purity of movement. Ballet and Jose' Limon's focus on the fluidity of the upper body added to the beauty of the dance.

Change was in the air.

Rose was six months shy of completing her thirty-second year. It was 1981. After performing her work to encouraging audiences the desire to go back to the world she had left behind took precedence. That summer she landed a part-time job as the booking agent for Jesse's River Journeys. It catapulted her one more step in her quest to leave the city life. Even further than the overriding fact that the sound of freeways every moment of her waking hours in the Bay Area. In her imagination they took on the sound of the Sweet River in Kindle City. Rose went on as many free day-trips to the Stanislaus River that her job allowed. Nature, the flow of the river and clear clean air beckoned her presence. Exhilarating, exquisite, refreshing and hypnotic was the river.

Ideas, many ideas of choreographing dances floated through her mind and body, but the time had come to end her position in the dance world before her chronic injuries and the jealous and predatory side of the human condition ended her dream.

One evening on a cold winter's day in Berkeley, Rose took Janet Carol's beginning ballet class at the Julia Morgan Center. It was to be her last class. No one knew who she was except the teacher. It was what she needed, to be anonymous when a decision that changed everything was about to happen.

When the class came to an end and a knowing that her dream was over welled up in her heart she thanked Janet from the depth of her soul.

Janet's response, "I'm sorry to hear the news. It will be a loss to the dance community, but I understand," eased the pain. She had experienced an injury plagued dance career as a performer, ending with the Oakland Ballet.

Rose's face, eyes and chest sank to the floor. "Thank you so much. I will miss you. I will miss all of this," her gaze moved to the now empty classroom.

Rose ambled out the door, tears running down her cheeks.

The years Rose was in the process of becoming a ballet trained modern dancer in unison with the five years she was an art model in the Bay Area were the most self-identifiable time of her life.

When she arrived home she took the longest bath she'd taken in years. She soaked and softened her entire body. Then, pumice stone in hand, she completely removed the multi-calloused areas on her feet that marked the spots that had protected them throughout her dance career. Years of doctoring her toes and the balls of her feet with antiseptic cream, wrapping them with gauze, followed by adhesive tape in order to protect them from further injury was over. One last time, Rose nursed her feet and allowed the cuts and floor burns to heal and never return.

Shaving down the hardened skin to the point that only a non-dancer would permit marked the end of a long-standing identity.

Rose's dog, Brandi, was lying on the bathroom rug. She was with her throughout the journey. She was there to hold and talk to when the adventures and heartaches of the dance world needed a tender and loyal creature.

Brandi ran parallel to Rose on the sidewalk while she rode her second five speed black Raleigh bike through the streets of Oakland and Berkeley to class. Then Brandi waited, tied up to a pole, next to her bike. As time went by and blessed with an adorable personality Brandi was allowed to lie under the desk at the Capezio Dance Theatre Shop when she helped customers. She rode along in Rose's VW Bug and then curled up in the back seat while she performed her responsibilities as an artist's model.

The luckiest, kindest gift that was bestowed upon Brandi was when she was invited to lay on the stair landing of the Shawl Anderson Modern Dance Center. For close to a decade, Brandi received endless hellos and pats from Rose's fellow dancers and teachers. Frank and Victor, generous and warmhearted, offered her a place in their world.

Dreams come true.

Part Four

I wanted to love someone so much that I cared about nothing else and other things seemed nonexistent, but I couldn't.

Work, friends, parents and the opinions of others were always there. Rose headed north in her now named Sammy, the 1968 VW Bug. After all that that car had done for her it needed a name. Her promise to herself to keep the car the rest of her life was in defiance to her father's disbelief in her. It was the only way that she could speak and do her truth and not get beat up. He had absolutely no power over her relationship with her car. Even in his death Rose couldn't let go of the evil surrounding that man.

Her grandfather's middle name was Samuel. Mother said he was a generous, independent and intelligent man. So Sammy it was. The car brought out the assertive maleness in Rose. It was the guy in her that not only got her where she needed to go, but away from where she needed not to be.

At thirty-two years old, Rose was still a beauty, single, unmarried and without children. After a day on the road she and her eleven year old dog, Brandi, landed in Briggs. It was a growing town located in the mountains and valleys of the most northern section of California. A remote self-sufficient town, people held a knowing of each other, but for the most part they left each other alone. Rose liked that, she liked that a lot. She needed to start over, be someone else and remake herself.

Her old friend Wendy, was a seasoned cocktail waitress at Smithy's, a bar and restaurant. She was caught up in the trawls of living in a rent-to-own house that she planned to buy and make it hers. Rose had stayed in touch with Wendy long after leaving the family home. The fact that she knew more about Rose than she sometimes wished was a bit disconcerting, but we need friends, friends that we don't have to explain ourselves to. It wasn't long before Rose rented the attic room at Wendy's that she had let her stay in to get her bearings. Though its walls were in serious need of repair, Wendy's house was in a sweet, quiet neighborhood completely the opposite of the questionable spots that Rose had endured in the Bay Area. There were no screaming kids, delinquent parents, ladies of the night, the pop, pop, pop of firearms, teenagers "making rubber" in stolen cars or ambulances and patrol cars screeching by.

Now in her late sixties, Rose's mother never let a phone call go by without stating her selfish needs, "When are you going to settle down, find a man and for once make me proud? Make me a grand-mother. Your child bearing years are coming to an end. Art's been married for ten years. He and his wife are devoted to their church, own a house and now have two boys."

Art, her once ally, hadn't kept in touch. "I'm not a letter writer." For all she knew he still thought of her as the little sister who had to scream at the top of her lungs for freedom from Luke or die a victim of rape.

Rose, wishing that she didn't need that women's approval and questioning herself as to why she chose to hand out her where-abouts so quickly responded "Mother, I danced in two companies and choreographed dances peopled liked. I'm still very capable of being self-employed. I have and will continue to make my way in life. I don't want to get married to please you. I won't have kids to make you proud. I must love the man I marry, know that he loves me and believe that he will be a good father to our children."

Then Mother stated in her all too familiar matter-of-fact tone, "Love doesn't mean much in the real world. Yes, you finally found something to do with your rootless life, but it was creative not practical. It's not ladylike to be self-employed and unmarried. Mimi wouldn't have it. You know that. Independence is not a desirable trait in a woman."

Holding onto all that she knew of women's rights, which was plenty, to be equal in the eyes of men, Rose stated with a calm self-assured tone that masked her sorrow, "That was so for you and your generation, you have said that often. I don't need to hear it. Stop hammering your ways on to my life. A life you haven't been a part of for decades. Besides, there're plenty of single, produc-tive women in the world. In fact I clearly remember you wanting that for yourself. If James were alive, hadn't drowned swimming across a swift river, you would have worked with him and your father. You would have married James not Father, become the intellectual you wanted to be and not been stuck at home doing for Father. Mother, it depends on who you talk to. Let me be." She couldn't hold back the tears that her mother couldn't see. She pulled her legs into her chest and hugged herself.

Silence echoed through the phone line. It was odd for her mother, a woman who always had something to say about most everything to sigh and then say, "And you're right about James. I loved him. You would've had pitch black hair, our lives would have been so different, but I worry. You're beyond the healthy child bearing age. Who's going to care for you when you are as old as me?"

Angry and frustrated, Rose shook her head, stuck her tongue out and then declared, "I don't know. How would I know? I am who I am. Stop trying to mold me into what you think I am supposed to be."

Mother caved, "Rose, I wish I had the emotional strength in the prime of my life that you have. You're independent, a very beautiful women. That can be dangerous. Please be careful."

As reassuring as she could be Rose responded, "Mother, try not to worry. Remember that when Art gives you the know-it-all speech about my not being able to take care of myself. Tell him that I'm doing just fine."

A sigh of resignation passed through the phone-line then Mother said, "OK dear. Good talking. Write soon. Stanley's right here. He wants me to say hello for him."

"Hi, back. Bye."

In a café only weeks after her arrival in Briggs, Rose met Dean. He was a gorgeous twenty-six years old with broad shoulders, medium build, dark-brown thick wavy hair and mustache, easy to tan, smooth muscles and hot. A radiant golden glow surrounded him with such fire. There was no stopping them from getting to know each other in ways so very new to him, but not to Rose.

For three months, every chance they got, they drove through the evergreen treed landscaped mountains and lush valleys of

Briggs and the surrounding communities. Sweet Brandi sat on her haunches in the truck bed of Dean's pale blue Chevy four-wheel drive truck with the wind in her face. Her days of waiting in the Bug, their room or tied up to a pole were over.

Dean was eye candy. When talk was exhausted they had unleashed sex in her hot and steamy attic. Then the all too familiar veil of truth lifted. She felt empty and hollow for having sex with him.

Rose knew when she met him that it wouldn't work out in the end. She was fading right before his eyes, but she thought she needed a solid relationship in her life. Even when her intuition screamed, "He's too dependent. He's a momma's-boy. Get scarce. He's going to dim your light and you are going to have to fight to turn it back on." She kept seeing him.

Her know-it-all, pushy old friend and housemate Wendy, couldn't resist chiming in, "He's got a job, is devoted to his family and downright traditional. You'd be a fool to let him go."

She kept seeing him.

Dean was persistent. Never failed to call when he said he would and had a steady job with a well-known and trusted contractor who paid on time. His boss was as demanding as Dean was of himself. They were a good match.

Dean could do most anything. He was a handyman. He painted cars. Give him a house plan and darn if he didn't follow it to the letter. He was a contractor in the making, the perfect mate, the perfect man. He didn't smoke. Rose needed to quit.

Rose was impressed. He just might satisfy her Mother. Maybe just maybe she'd leave her alone, except he wanted to get married and have kids. She didn't want kids. The world was over populated. Never did and still didn't believe it was a necessary station in life, being a wife and mother. Rose was scared to death of it. No adults who were capable of teaching her the skills of parenting came to her aid. The amoral relationships her parents had introduced her to, put her at odds with the idea of coupling.

Dean's great Aunt Isabelle and Aunt Betty lived nearby. They got under her skin in a most adoring way. They were sweet ladies, rugged and self-sufficient, her kind of women.

But then there was Dean's mother. That woman was a neat freak. She questioned Dean as to why in the world his girlfriend needed that half-an-hour alone before hanging out with her and her other children to easy her nerves and feel centered with exercise. Her driving need to manipulate the comings and goings of anyone within her reach, in Rose's eyes, was stifling. Every single time she and Dean drove the five hundred miles to visit his childhood home. Rose was plagued with visions of what might be.

Try as she did to appease Dean's mother, doing as she wished when she wished it. It never seemed to work for more than a moment.

Sharing one of Aunt Betty's delicious homemade chocolate chip cookies in her kitchen while Dean and his cousin Jeffery worked on a car in the garage she shook her head and said, "Rose I usually stay out of this kind of thing, but you're a sweet girl, which by the way doesn't mean a damn thing to Dean's mom. No one will ever be good enough for her son. Take my word for it. She's my sister-in-law. I know that woman."

Dean had this unrelenting need to be perfect in his work. Needed to change and dominate his parent's home, make-a-new this or do that around their house. They never allowed him to do much which made it even more important for him to do for them. Rose didn't see the need to change his family's life style. She wanted to focus on her own. She just hung out watching and listening, wishing Dean would let it go. She wanted to go to the ocean. It was only a walk away from their home in San Francisco. Ships and sail boats drifted by, surfers and bathers covered the shores. She wanted to be one of them, collect shells and dive under the waves, swim to shore and allow her body to soak up the sun. But Dean was focused on the chores he thought needed doing at his parent's home. Rose felt invisible.

One evening, on their way back to Briggs an imaginary big red flag wafted by her face with such force that Rose declared, "Dean you're so much more drawn into and controlled by your family than I. I'm not the person for you. I don't want to get married. I don't visit my family as you do. It's not going to work."

Dean stopped the car. "It will be OK you'll see," with a hug and a kiss.

It was all it took. Rose was lonely and ashamed of whom she thought she was and couldn't shake it for more than a few hours each day, those precious hours that she was alone.

Against all odds, Dean and Rose bought land as two unmarried individuals and built a house. Their cat Lulu, and dogs Sam and Ufda came along. She had a dream to own a horse and have the land to house it for the rest of its life. He wanted to build a house. She wanted a place to raise the horse, find peace of mind, be in the open clean air and not have to pack her bags. To her, the house was a necessary material procession. It was his domain. Mother gave Rose half of the down payment. She wanted her daughter settled. For once in Rose's life her own mother was on her side.

Although Dean and Rose had enjoyed a delightful and adventurous sex life, it was not to be Rose's desires alone that clung to him. Her need to protect and nurture her dog Ufda and horse Lana, kept Rose from leaving the house and property. Staying with Dean on their land was the foundation Rose had to have to fulfill her promise to her horse.

Unyielding in her need to have some power over her life, Rose supported herself. She took on housecleaning jobs. An effective and efficient worker she never failed to get work. By organizing a yard-work business she was the employer and the employee. It was all hers. She loved that.

I hoofed the mile to and from school, but I was never really in a hurry. It was the possibilities of connections that intrigued me the most. My friends, neighbors and the animals along the way, especially the bees buzzing working the flowers near the side-walk got my attention. The bees never frightened me. Their yellow and black pudgy little bodies were fascinating. If my parents ever wondered where I was all they had to do was walk or drive my steady habitual path to and from school. I'd be lost in the rest-less focus of my tiny friends.

Always ready to appreciate and assist Dean in the building of the house, Rose did her part. At the end of each day when she had put in her hours at work outside the home she never failed to thank the crew working on her their house. To then clear up the debris for the next day's work.

During Christmas and winter seasons, she was a full-timer in the busiest shop in town. It kept her in a position of power. She wasn't about to give Dean the upper hand financially.

Dean and Rose dealt with the county's intense critiquing way to complete the building of the house. When alone at the building department, Rose went face to face with those in charge addressing the rigid safety building codes of the county. She kept her cool, believed and understood the rules of construction and then relayed the information to Dean and friends for the next step.

Within a year, they got signed off.

To complete the cosmetics of their home, Rose contributed the professional house painting skills she'd acquired in the Bay Area when she needed a bit more cash than the art modeling jobs offered.

She was a trimmer and roller. She was secure with her skill and had no problem assuming the role of house painter for their home. She painted the whole house inside and out. The building contractor Jim needed some rooms painted in his home. They exchanged labor. It was a great benefit to all involved. Or so Rose thought. But to Dean and his parents it wasn't as important as what he was doing. Rose's emotional and physical support was never good enough to satisfy his parent's ideal of an appropriate mate for Dean. Rose felt the pain of the unspoken undercurrent. Dean as hard as he tried couldn't shake the question. Were they right?

But he had said and continued to say, "I love you. Don't worry everything will work out."

But for Rose it was the fact that she had promised her horse that she'd never have to live anywhere else. A ten year old, flea-bit-gray Arabian mare with a charcoal-gray mane and a blond tail that almost hit the ground was a beauty. That horse was her kid, her child, her responsibility. She was Lana's third guardian. There was no way that she wouldn't keep her promise. Rose was stubborn that way.

Dean's uncles, aunts, sisters and cousins showed-up uninvited. No call, letter of request, nothing. It gnawed on Rose incessantly.

She put on a happy face, but had to speak her truth, "Dean they need to call first. It's rude to just stop by unannounced. It never happened at my house."

"Rose, that's the way they are. My parents have an open door policy. It's the way it is."

Open door policy, those words squeezed her gut tight. So tight that she couldn't say a damn word until all the work and the hope for a secure life and her will to survive demanded her to. Her eyes welled up with tears then she burst out, "Your parents never come by. If we see them it's at your aunt's house or theirs. It's everyone else. It's my house too. With Mother's help, I paid for half of everything and still do. I have a say here." Then uncontrollable buckets of tears flowed down her beet-red face.

"Well, O.K. I'll talk to them. But it's not going to go over well."

Dean came closer, offered her a hug, but Rose couldn't bear it. She stomped off.

Dean made a call to his parents. Weeks went by. As it turned out the two people, his parents, who chose not to visit at all were prompting the others to drop by and then relaying the news good, bad or indifferent. She had little to offer him in consolation, much less experience. She felt an uneasy sorrow for Dean. To him it was who they were.

Dean had put hours and hours of himself into the first house he and Rose built with their friends. It was not unusual. In fact it was understood for her not to be visited by her family. But Dean grew distant when his parents, without a word, stopped calling. Messages to Dean, not Rose, came from his parents through the aunts.

Then one afternoon, Aunt Brenda cornered Rose. It was one of those visits that she was kind enough to call ahead and ask. They were alone, far away from anyone when a whisper struggled out of her, "That woman didn't like me being married to her brother. She made underhanded remarks behind my back. She never invited me to events unless there was no way out of it. Don't take it too personal. She's a possessive controlling bitch."

Rose didn't want to hear that. They'd just finished the house, the house she thought she was going to live in for the rest of her life.

So there she was embedded with Dean's family. The one person, his mother, whom he was bound to the most, didn't like her, wouldn't like her, no matter what. She wasn't his mother and had no intensions of becoming her for Dean no matter how much he wished.

To Rose's profound relief and surprise, to many members of his family it made sense. In fact they too were that way, always making arrangements between themselves. It was Dean's parents who had the open door policy. They had the upper hand worlds away in their spotless upper class neighborhood.

Rose was drawn more and more to her job, the chores, her horse and dog. It left little in the way of affection for Dean. He and his parent's lives were snarled together like a bee caught in a spider's web. Rose couldn't let on to the death grip that she witnessed every time they called. It put her back in the all too familiar limbo of her life.

They worked to pay the bills. They traveled together, camped together alone with friends and spooned after the heat of passion subsided. How could Rose fight the shame of her childhood and be herself in the mist of Dean's opinionated controlling mother. Wasn't she the one that should matter more to Dean than his mother. But she didn't and that hurt? It hurt a lot.

On Labor Day a year after they finished the house, Rose was scheduled to clean the Briggs Fire Station. It was a holiday for many, but not her. She parked her car as usual, opened the truck bay door, walked into the kitchen about to remove her jacket when a faint meow came from outside the kitchens back door. On the cement floor huddled between two garbage cans was a skinny little kitten. She immediately went over to the nearby restaurant and gas station to find the owner. After much conversation with a kind woman named Sally, who lived next to the Fire Station, she promised to come over and take a look at the kitten as soon as she got some time. Rose found some food that she thought the kitten just might eat and made up a bed just outside the back door in the old sink using a dish towel. She hoped the little guy would eat and get some rest. Much to her dismay, the kitten wouldn't eat a thing. She petted it as much as her emotions allowed. After all it wasn't hers. She shouldn't get involved, but the cat's purr was so loud, its head pushed hard against her hand. It surely must belong to someone. But it was so boney, wouldn't eat and then began to throw-up, seriously indicating the presence of round worms. The cat's eyes, nose and ears were full of dirt, mites and puss and its lungs were congested. Rose found it hard to believe the owners understood the health needs of the little thing.

Feeling the responsibilities of her job, Rose began to clean. She was wishing and hoping someone, somewhere would help this tiny creature that had just come into her life.

Sally arrived. She took a good look at the kitten, told Rose who owned it and what she thought of its situation, "It's bad. If you have any desire to take this kitten home with you, please do. The owners obviously don't take care of it. He'd be much better off with you."

Rose considered all the times she'd followed through with her duties in life. Her taking this kitten would have to be a secret. She was about to kidnap him. Her desire to do the right thing weighed heavy on her heart. There was not simply one right thing to do.

Doors locked, hall clean, Rose's affinity with animals propelled her back to the sick feline. The kitten was still there. It was in a deep sleep in the old sink. Her hand scooped up the not more than a pound kitten. He woke up with a purr and eyes full of endless hope. She wondered what life had in store for her and her family of fine furry friends once the new kitten became a part of their lives.

The sweet abandoned kitten was given the name Fireball. Rose had heard that it was discovered at an old abandoned house that the fire department had burned down. Rose play chased him into the kitchen from the living room. He found refuge behind the washing machine only to come out as soon as Rose's voice changed to a silly sound. Then quickly his little self came out from behind, purring as loud as can be. His name stayed Fireball as he grew into a large white tabby, but as the days went by and his true personality came out, his name changed into a suitable Sire. Not only did it rhyme with Fire, it was truly him. He was slow moving, thoughtful and full of affection. He had long, luscious hair and loving eyes that were as green as the newly sprouted spring grass. A cat full of the elegance of the Sire, he became the father of the furry family, wise, tolerate and warm.

When the dogs were off being silly, adventurous or foolish, Sire sat at home either on Rose's saddle for Lana, on the porch railing or in the house awaiting a meal or a pet. His most energetic move was to wait for Rose at the bottom of the stairs in hopes that she would chase him to his food on top of the washing machine.

Rose had befriended the plumber's wife Sara, months before her very first child was due to be born. For the duration of Nate's contribution to the building of Dean and Rose's home Sara had left Nate off to then return after the day was done. She was reserved with her information, but Rose could see and feel that Sara was struggling with the prospect of becoming a mother.

After completing the morning chores on the eve of May, Rose went to keep her pregnant friend, Sara, company. When she arrived she found out that days before, she and her husband Nate had rushed to the hospital believing their baby was on its way out, but the timing was off. The doctor stopped the process, assuming the baby would cook a bit longer. Sara's entire body was fidgeting on the couch. Her shaky voice sent chills into the depths of Rose. Labor pains bellowed throughout the entire room.

Rose was stunned, in disbelief that what she suspected was needed from her surfaced. Was she going to have to call 911 or drive them through the river canyon on a two lane road for twenty miles to the hospital?

Sara cried out, "Do you think I should call the doctor?"

Deliberate, Rose uttered, "Yes, it will make you feel better."

Momentarily reassured, Sara picked up the phone inches from her side and called, listened and then she slammed the phone down. "You know what that damn doctor said?"

Scared out of her mind to hear the outcome Rose replied, "No. What?"

Sara's entire body flushed with a burning anger. She struggled to lift her heavy load, grasped and twisted her dress over her belly then flung herself back onto the couch, "Take some more of the pills your doctor prescribed and call me if the pains come back. Those guys don't get it."

They tried to relax. The phone rang twice. Her mom and a neighbor, Jackie, called to check up. Sara kept the calls short and reassuring.

Labor pains slammed back. The intensity was far beyond the limitations of medication, Rose's experience and Sara's comfort zone.

Would Sara make a second call to the doctor? Rose had to wait. It was not her choose to make, but she wanted her to, prayed that she would.

Sara had had it. She wasn't going to take suggestions from anyone, authority or not. She stated with fury, "We're in charge. We're going to the hospital period."

Logic embedded itself in a panic-stricken Rose who then focused on the task at hand.

Sara and Nate had a communication strategy, but she didn't want to let on. She was frantic, "Rose please call Nate. He knows my voice too damn well. He'll know how scared I am."

Nate was at work not far from the hospital.

Rose faked a calm and in control exterior. She labored her way through the numbers to connect to Nate's one-way communication cell-phone, "Nate, Sara and I are leaving for the hospital. Be there as soon as you can."

This position, a position Rose had chose not to have any part of throughout her life was placed upon her. The responsibilities she felt for Sara and her baby was of the utmost. She couldn't allow fear and inexperience to hinder the birth of this child.

Sara lumbered to the bathroom. Her water broke.

From the toilet seat Sara screeched, "Shoes, where are my shoes?"

"I'll look."

"The birth-bag is next to the door."

"Got it, forget the shoes," Rose declared.

Sara steamed with frustration when she failed in her attempt to sidestep and hip-hoist herself up onto the passenger seat of her CRV. "Damn it. Shit. Now what?"

Rose glanced over to her car. She dreaded driving her dear old car to the hospital, but she had to resign herself to the truth. In a placid tone she said, "Looks like we'll have to take the Bug."

Pissed at the world, Sara yelled, "That old car. It won't make it."

Conflicted and close to saying the hell with it all, Rose firmly stated, "You got any better ideas?"

Bedraggled and exhausted, Sara shook her head then struggled with her swollen with child body to Rose's car, maneuvered her seat back to its limits then jimmied herself into place for the long drive.

Rose pulled the emergency switch on. Contractions came and went every four to five minutes.

Rose's friends had called her a "sensible driver" with a laugh, snicker and "for God's sake" tone for years. It served her well that day.

Rose's aging car, in serious need of a tune-up, was forced to go way beyond the call of duty. Her thoughts and feelings were all over the map. She had both hands on the wheel, but when she could one made its way to Sara's thigh in reassurance.

It had been raining and hailing on and off all morning. They swung left and right and back again easing down to the approach of the river canyon bridge. The sun blazed through the clouds' fractured spaces. Spectacular sparkles of green shone up and down the oak and pine tree covered cannon walls. Fluffy white clouds, blue skies and a rainbow that stretched from one side of the ravine to the other gave them a moment in time to go beyond the chaos. They held their words, closed their minds to any distraction for the twenty miles except to acknowledge the sky, rainbow and billowing clouds.

Out of the gorge ominous charcoal clouds jumped into Rose's heart. Its hard and fast rhythm, a wish that they could fly to the bed that would bring the baby here dominated her. Speeding down the last, long, straight six mile stretch from their destination Sara's intense frustration put Rose's determination to do what she had taken on to the test.

Sara's legs were wide open and extended. Her full pelvis, the tension to release anything that would, a situation that couldn't be fixed by them she yelled, "Hurry up. What are you doing, forty miles an hour? Get this heap of tin moving. Cars are passing us. It's coming."

Rose divided focus, drive, pray, drive, pray kept her moving. "It's not the right time little one. The car is no place to be born. You will need far more than your mom and me to be a healthy being and we're all that you have right now. Please wait just a little longer."

It was damn cool. The windows wide open, Rose's gloveless hands stiff and frozen solid were wrapped around the wheel.

Sara hot, short tempered and sweating profusely pulled in her power and then screeched, "Speed up, damn it!"

Even toned Rose responded, "My car can't go any faster."

"Are you sure?"

"Yes." Rose wasn't going to give way to Sara's desires for anything. She refused to question her own judgment. If they had to stop and flag down someone to help, then so be it.

They pulled up to the hospital. Nate was standing out in the cold hard hail. He ran in front of the car, leading them to the entrance. Relieved beyond words, Rose parked the car, her job done.

Rose and Nate bookended Sara as she trudged to the receptionist's desk, they waited. Sara was unable to relax, but her gratitude seeped into Rose when she said, "Do you want to watch?"

Rose thought, "You've got to be kidding," but said, "Well a, yes I'd be honored," surprised and touched. No one had ever trusted her with a life experience like this before.

Within the cocoon of the hospital, people were moving about here and there. The hospital staff was inundated with paperwork and phone calls. Absolutely no one was making eye contact with them.

Holding his wife up and completely infolded by what was happening, Nate repeated over and over again, "Are you OK Babe?"

Frustration was building up in Sara. She glared into Nate's eyes and then only because she was in the hospital, mustered up a reserved, but intense response, "No I'm not! What's wrong with these people, can't they see me?"

That instant a nurse offered Sara a wheelchair, pushed her into the delivery room. Nate was at her side. Rose followed a bit bewildered, but proud of a job well done she held her head up high and observed the workings of the professionals.

Sara's doctor was off that day. The hospital had little equipment for premature deliveries. The doctor on duty suggested medicating Sara once again in hopes of holding off the birth.

After neither Sara nor Nate could muster up the courage to speak. Rose said, "Please, help her. It didn't work the first, second or third time. What makes you think it will work this time? It's not working. That's why we're here."

They gave it to her anyway. Fifteen minutes went by. The pain persisted, came back with a power so strong that the doctors and nurses couldn't ignore.

After a frantic reiteration of the days events the head nurse ordered, "Wheel her into the Delivery Room now."

The doctors and nurses were tired from bringing five babies into the world that very morning, nonetheless they took on the challenge with experience and empathy. An oxygen face mask was place on Sara's swinging beet red face. Nate replaced it over and over again. A metal rolling lipped table was full of sterilized utensils, odd shaped scissors and spoons and knives and a rolling incubator was in a corner. Sara's focus and determination coupled with Nate's attentiveness to his family's needs filled the room. Rose felt out of place. She loved Nate and Sara, but was not among the circle of intellect.

I was holding up the walls.

Then the doctor looked to Rose, "Need a job?"

A bit unnerved she responded, "OK."

"It's simple, but it's one less thing for us to do. Note the time of birth."

Sara's mother called. Rose was assigned the task of talking to her. She had never met her, but she was it.

The second after Rose announced her name and her relationship to Sara. Sara's mother blurted out, "How's the baby? How's Sara? What happened? Why is she there? The baby's not due for months."

"They're doing fine. You've got a strong-minded daughter. The nurses hooked up heart-monitors to Sara and the baby. I heard their pulses loud and clear."

Rose was grateful to have honest and most of all positive information to relay.

A couple of hours passed. The baby crowned. Then when the neck came into view, with a visual of the umbilical cord wrapped around its neck, special precautions were instigated to safe-guard Sara and her baby. It was out of Rose's sight, but she could see and hear the lightning speed orders, eye contact, hands on work of the professionals and the unrelenting push of Sara.

At exactly 1:40 pm little girl Sheri was born. She was deep purple, crinkled, a mere three and a half pounds and crying life into her lungs. The attending nurse wanted to snatch her up. She hovered, her arms stretched out inches away from baby Sheri, but Sara insisted that she be allowed to look at and hold her newborn to her heart. "You're the most beautiful baby in the world. I love you."

Rose was deeply moved. She began to cry quiet tears. She was humbled, relieved and exhausted when she moved just a bit too close to the rolling metal table full of sterilized utensils. The attending nurse sent daggers into Rose's eyes. Rose hadn't meant to touch anything and believed the stress of the day put the rage into the nurse's soul.

In seconds, baby Sheri was placed deep inside the protective glass oxygen filled incubator.

The attending doctor locked eyes with Rose, "The afterbirth is stuck to your friend's uterus. It's not a pleasant situation for anyone. It's time for you to go."

Rose left the hospital filled with heavy emotions. Worries lingered the long drive home.

Hours later Rose called, "How are you all doing?"

Nate laughed with an undertone of great appreciation, "No. How are you doing?"

"Well, I'm numb, thankful we got to the hospital safe and sound and extremely happy you are all doing so well."

Spoken in truth and honesty Nate said, "We're glad you were there for us. Thanks."

"Your welcome, I'll see you soon. Bye for now." Enriched by the experience, Rose set the receiver down, looked around at her world, a world she was grateful to go back to, but not that very minute. For a while she pondered the morning's events and couldn't quite believe what she had done, seen and lived through with her friends.

Soon after Dean arrived home, she shared her day with him. He was very proud of her, but couldn't help saying with a tone of worry in his voice, "Didn't that old car of yours need a tune-up?"

"Yep."

"The Gods were on your side."

"Yes, indeed. They sure were."

"So what's for dinner girl?"

Sara and baby Sheri needed a great deal of special care for weeks to come.

The question, could I handle an emergency, be useful and not panic were answered that day.

Part Five

I was empty from waiting for Dean to put me first.

Icy roads and hailing skies of one winter night saw Dean and Rose with their neighbor, Jordan Rose wedged in the middle of the trucks cab, driving to their first fire department training. Rose was a strong, athletic, forty year old assertive woman. It was in her blood, the power of her body. It was what she could count on.

The sidewalks that ran up and down West Drive was my playground as soon as my little legs and arms could muscle me up, down and around the endless obstacles of imaginary people, shrubs, pumps, overgrown tree roots that pushed up the sidewalk and cracks that the aging cement provided. The sidewalk was quite steep up at the end of the street then eased into a slow decline halfway down the hill. Rest assured, when my roller skates caught a crack or my balance was lost, if for only for a moment, I received many a skinned knee, elbow, cheek and hand. I required much iodine from Mother's medicine cabinet. Boy, did it sting, but it was so worth it. Full of pride, I bragged to the neighborhood kids. My scrapes, scabs and bandages were proof of my bravery. My brothers and I would hop on our red wagon and coast down the hill to the safety of someone's lawn, if all went well, but a crash and burn was highly possible. We all survived, only to climb all the way up to the top of West Drive and do it all over again.

The trainings were led by Chief Jim Brady. Within the last five years political heat had spread throughout the department and rumors of loss of personnel and a great need to replenish got Dean and Rose's attention. Some felt the chief was incompetent, but Rose's egalitarian mind was full of idealism and blind to the social structure of the department.

Jim, as he preferred they call him, was forty years old and had twenty years of experience in the fire service. He was a member of the Briggs Volunteer Fire Department long before Rose entered the department. He was also a certified firefighting instructor. A humanitarian, married to one of the board members and self-employed, his organizational talents, dedication and public relation skills were among his strengths. Rose appreciated his emphasis on teamwork, self-reliance in the heat of battle and the proper use of fire equipment whether used or new. He made sure the department's wildland and structure fire gear and medical bags, slightly worn or donated were repairable and kept clean. The medical equipment and fire apparatus were up-to-date and ready on a moments notice.

The Chief Jim Brady shared his philosophy when and if necessary, "There is no such thing as just a volunteer, especially in this line of work. We are professionals."

In late winter and early spring of 1991, Jim trained twenty new recruits in advanced first-aid and firefighting. Wildland firefighting and medical emergencies were emphasized.

The seventy-square-mile district housed wide-spread structures nestled within the pine, oak and madrone trees along with scotch broom, buck brush, manzanita and poison oak bushes. The numerous rutted dirt roads were squeezed tight into tunnels of encroaching shrubs. The potential for a structure fire to explode into a wildland fire was high to absolute. Mutual-aids overlapped into the immediate neighboring districts. The 911 emergency calls were estimated at two-hundred and fifty per year. On average the scene of an emergency was a half-hour away from the assistance of an ambulance, law enforcement and the neighboring fire departments' equipment and crew. Except during fire season when CDF was stationed in the district. Otherwise, Briggs Volunteer Fire Department was on its own until they could let go of the complete responsibility of an emergency or share the load.

Mother, now in her late seventies, was visiting. The winter's rain and snow had soaked the land making it safe to have structure fire training down the road from Rose's home. She needed to go. Mother was invited by the chief. She declined but was oddly supportive of her daughter's choice to be an emergency responder, "You were always calm and collected during our family squabbles."

Rose was glad to get time away from her on the seemingly long visit of four days, her limit. Mother often said, "Like fish, after four days you stink."

Not until her older brother Art's phone call weeks after the visit, Rose didn't know that he'd attempted to force Mother to stay home. She wasn't well. She came to Rose's home to assert her willful personality, hoping to find the dutiful daughter, the subservient servant. Rose was done with it.

As always Mother had a book, was caught up in it and hard to communicate with. Words had a strange power over Rose. She felt inadequate, stupid when she didn't understand them. Whenever she needed to pull Mother away from her book, just to talk, she felt queasy and anxious. She had for years prayed to no avail for her mother's addiction to dissipate into love and protection for her, but Mother's behavior was ingrained. Books were her life's blood. Rose understood, but that didn't make her not dream of the mothers in story books.

Frustration mounting and time shortening, Rose let loose, "Mom, remember when you allowed that man to rape me for three years?"

She shrugged.

"That's what he did. You didn't believe me then and you still don't. Why, I don't get it?"

Mother's eyes lowered and she laid her book on her lap.

"You believed him when he said I liked it. I didn't. I yelled, "No" hundreds of times. Art heard it. Stanley heard it. Admit it, it was wrong, admit it!"

Silence, nothing but silence came from Mother.

"Mom it was wrong, admit it. You and Dad were wrong for allowing him to come into our home. Admit it."

Once again, nothing whatsoever came from the woman who had brought such turmoil into Rose's life. Then a very odd thing came to the surface. Mother's face rolled into a childish spoiled innocence. It unnerved Rose. Then in a flash of knowing she realized the truth. Mother wanted Luke and had won him. Rose was simply a means with a short intermission then a path to her desires. It was so easy to put the blame on the twelve year old Rose for bringing shame to the family circle that day when she ran through the front door into their yard and screamed the truth for all the neighbors to hear. Mother had eliminated the memory of abuse to ease her participation in her only daughter's forsaken youth.

Mother's last words before she headed home, "Rose you were always so calm when the fights blew up. I think your choice to be a member of your local fire department is a good one," fell into a part of Rose's mind that held hidden pieces of her childhood for decades. That calmness that her mother believed to be effective was full of reluctance for Rose, a reluctance to speak anything at all for fear of her life.

Rose believed in herself. She had been a modern and ballet dancer in her twenties and understood the mechanics of the body. Her experience with dance injuries came from not only numerous dance injury classes, but also from the healing of the back and leg sprains and strains personally sustained. Teamwork was a skill she acquired from being a member of two dance companies and working in the public. Rose knew these skills would come in handy caring for patients in a variety of scenarios as well as fighting the onset of a wildland or structure fire. From the beginning of her time in the department she was very aware of her abilities and weaknesses and vowed to never stay on the scene of a long-lived fire within the district.

After Rose had responded to multiple emergency calls and worked in close proximity to the rescue captain, Debbie Skinner and the EMT instructor and retired paramedic, Patty Steel, they supported Rose's desire to become an Emergency Medical Technician.

Patty Steel had a strong resolve, "There are plenty of stupid EMTs out there. I don't want to see or hear about any of them coming out of my class."

Rose had absolutely no problem with Patty's resolve. She shared it. But to her disappointment in the fall of 1991, she barely passed the twelve week EMT certification class.

Within that same month Rose received the disheartening news of her mother's demise. Now, down in southern California, Art, Stanley and Dean were picking up a U-Haul. While the men were away doing last minute odds and ends she meandered outside and then sat herself down on the steps at the end of the cement walkway. Gut wrenching memories of time spent in the family's home were running through her mind and body when a woman in her seventies shuffled up the sidewalk. She stopped on the property-line. Rose didn't make sense of her abrupt halt until she recognized the woman. The loving protective and familiar smile melted into Rose's soul.

"Mrs. South?"

"Yes, Rose, how are you? I heard your mother died. Is that why you are here?"

"Yes, it is."

This woman, from her childhood, chose to come up to her. Rose was surprised and so very happy, but pensive to see one of the most important neighbors that she had when life in this house, a house of endless trauma, almost killed her spirit. Mrs. South had the heart and strength to help when no one else would take a step beyond their own lives.

Moving to the far edge of the step and then softly patting it, Rose said, "Would you like to sit down and visit for a bit?"

To upright herself Mrs. South pushed her cane into the sidewalk, shook her head and looked only with her eyes at the house across the street. Then she looked at Rose to state, "Stanley won't let me come closer."

Rose shifted her weight in a move to get up.

"Don't!"

Her body sinking in despair Rose held her emotions in check to respond, "Why?"

Sweet Mrs. South, barely able to stand said with clarity, "Dear Rose, your brother frightens me. I wish I could hug you, but he's become a bitter and belligerent man since you left. He believes I'm the reason you left."

Sincerely and from the depth of her Rose let out a deep breath and then said, "If that is so, I am forever grateful to you for choosing to do and say something on my behalf then and now."

Mrs. South nodded and then shifted her vulnerable balance to say, "Thank you, I thought I helped, but I never knew for sure. I needed to hear it from you. It's time for me to get back inside. I'm having health problems. My caregiver would be upset with me if she found out that I was outside. A few neighbors noticed you the last couple of days collecting things. With the men gone, this was my only chance to say hello and see how you are doing."

Rose's eyes filled with tears, "Thank you so much! You saved my life. Here's a hug from my heart." It cut deep. They were not allowed to express themselves openly, but Rose wouldn't put the dear lady's life in any kind of danger. Stanley was lost in time and had grown into an erratic hot tempered man. His social skills were not to be trusted and she was no long there to soften his blows.

She forced herself back inside. Within half an hour Dean, Art and Stanley were back. Rose's share was loaded up. Things that meant more than money, Mimi's antique corner table, an oriental rug, her beloved tea and saucer sets and the Wizard of Oz books that she read to Mother then to them, Mimi's treasures. It was time to get back on the road.

On the long trip home, Rose told Dean of Mrs. South's act of kindness many years ago, but it wasn't something he could identify with. Nonetheless Mrs. South soothed her in ways she never forgot.

Months later, Rose called Stanley. It was miles and miles away from his world on West Dr. and very safe for her to say, "I'm calling regarding my conversation with Mrs. South."

He declared, "I don't talk to her."

"Stanley I need you to know that I love, respect and am grateful to that woman."

According to Stanley he never said a word to Mrs. South about her conversation. Nor did he mention her to Rose every again. She died less than a year later.

That loving woman meant the world to me.

I propelled myself into action. It was the best
way for me to forget.

In the spring of 1992 Rose retook the EMT test and aced it.

Dean worked full-time. He was frequently in the district, but unavailable or out-of-district. Rose now worked part-time as a teacher's aide and an overall sub for the district's elementary school and never failed to do her personalized workout most days. Twice a week come rain or shine or snow she rode Lana with her personally soft-hand trained Queensland heeler-Labrador cross dog Ufda, trailing along. She continued her full-time job during the holiday season as a sales clerk for the busiest retail store in town a half hour drive away. But for ten months out of the year she had half the day and all night to choose to respond to any given call. She was keen on it and poured her heart and soul into the emergency services. Rose's passionate desire to help humanity drove her. Knowing that she would arrive on the scene to soothe the fears and anxiety of mankind fed the humanitarian in her.

When the summer of 1992 rolled around, Rose experienced her first vehicle accident as a rural district, medical bag carrying EMT.

As Dean and Rose loaded up the truck to go to town, Dean suggested that they put their medical bag in the back, "Just in case."

"Sure why not, we'll be back in our district in a couple of hours."

Errands done, they were on their way home. One mile north of the south fork of the river canyon bridge they were stopped in their tracks when half-dozen vehicles haphazardly parked up and down the road.

One of the panic-stricken citizens pointed to their vehicle I.D. plate and announced, "They're Fire and Rescue."

With a completely unfamiliar reluctance Dean said, "Rose, we're out of our district. If we stop and help we're responsible for the outcome."

"Dean I'm an EMT. You're a first-responder. We have a brand-new medical bag in the truck. This is what we're trained to do."

Confused, but nonetheless executing a plan of action, the Good Samaritans had made vital decisions concerning the accident that happened only minutes before. Two men shouted directions to the oncoming traffic. A heavy duty truck carrying a large roll of electrical cable sat sideways, undamaged. The driver's front door faced uphill in the middle of the right-hand lane. The truck driver, a tall slim man in his late thirties, was disoriented, pacing, bent-over, pressing his hands to his forehead pleading, "Oh God, did I kill her? Is she OK? Is she OK? Please someone go down and help her."

The duty to act compelled every move Rose made. She walked with deliberateness over to the truck driver scanning his body for any possible injuries. There was nothing to indicate that anything was wrong with him physically. "Sir, I'm an EMT with the Briggs Volunteer Fire Department. Are you dizzy? Did you lose consciousness before or after you hit the vehicle?"

"No, No, I'm fine. Please take care of her. I was driving too fast when I took the curve. I went over the double line. It's my fault."

"Sir, I'm glad you're OK."

Four fear-paralyzed citizens pointed, looking down the hill. A car caught and cushioned by trees and shrubs was sitting upright with its backside pointing down about ten yards below the road.

Rose shouted, "Has anyone climbed down the hill?"

A frozen wide-eyed man responded, "No, only the guy standing over there by his truck knows what happened."

Dean rushed passed Rose fingering his hands into sterilized rubber gloves then climbed down the steep terrain. Medical bag in hand, feet first on her rear end, Rose followed him halfway down the hill. Dean eased himself into the back seat of the car behind the woman, identified himself, wrapped his hands around her neck and jaw to keep her spine steady and asked her name. Her eyes were wide open, rapid movements back and forth, up and down. She babbled. She was alive.

The engine was running. Beautiful soft, soothing music was playing on her cassette player. Rose smelled gasoline.

Dean said, "Rose, turn off the engine. We don't need to add a vehicle fire to the mix."

The car appeared to be steady. Rose was tempted to climb inside, but her weight alone could tip the precarious balance they were banking on. "Go for it. I must stay outside the car."

In the kindest voice Dean said, "I need to turn off your car. When I do, I'm sorry to say, it will end your beautiful music. We're worried a car fire might hamper our ability to help you."

The unidentified woman nodded.

Rose opened the medical bag and took out the run-sheet to document the vital information. The woman appeared to be in her late twenties or early thirties. She was beautifully dressed in shades of ocean-blue and plum-burgundy cotton and silk. She was laying downhill head first in the driver's seat. The steering wheel was almost up against her chest, no blood, nothing to indicate injury was apparent. Rose put her hand up to her mouth as if holding a container of alcohol, shrugged her shoulders and then tilted her head. Was she driving under the influence of alcohol? Rose needed to know. Dean shook his head. To confirm, there were no open containers in or near the car.

Again Dean asked, "What is your name?"

Through a veil of mumbles and a desperate attempt to squirm out of her seat she said, "Kathy. Who are you? What do you want?"

They understood her. Rose was elated.

Rose shouted out, "Dean, if the car moves get your ass out of there," and then thought "Shit, he's at least fifty pounds heavier than I am! It should be me in the car, but it can't be both of us."

"I will. Hand me the C-collar and the non re-breather bag-valve mask with the oxygen tank on fifteen liters."

From the medical bag Rose pulled out the oxygen tank, set it in the ready-to-use position, removed a bag-valve mask from its plastic container, picked out the correct C-collar then handed them to him. Dean administered the oxygen and placed the C-collar around Kathy's neck. Rose documented the vital information that they had gathered so far.

Tightness in her belly didn't allow her to stop thinking, "There's something wrong I can feel it, but what?"

And then it hit her, "AIRWAY, AIRWAY, first, always first don't forget." Her EMT teacher's voice repeating loud and clear in Rose's mind, she dropped the run-sheet.

From her perch halfway between the car and the road she called out, "Dean, we're having a hard time understanding her. It looks like she has a broken jaw. Blood might be dripping down her throat and clogging it up."

Rose said, "Kathy can you feel your feet?"

"Yes," agitated, but the tone of her voice had softened.

"Excellent. Dean, slowly push her forward."

"Why? It might injure her spine."

"Yes it might, but we need to find out if there's a problem with her airway."

He removed one hand from her jaw and neck, put it on the center of her back and pushed. "Kathy can you still feel your feet?"

She nodded.

"Dean, push her further."

"OK, but it's going to be impossible to hold her."

Thick heavy bright red blood and broken teeth streamed out of her disfigured mouth. Holding onto Kathy's back with one hand, Dean pulled a large pillow and blanket from the back seat. He shimmed them behind her. It did the job, held her in place and freed his hands.

The blood stopped flowing from Kathy's mouth. Dean gently loosened the C-collar from around her neck. Using only his fingers, he methodically shifted her jaw to its correct position and slipped the C-collar back under her jaw. From outside the driver's seat of the car, Rose assisted Dean in the removal of the blood clogged oxygen facemask. They replaced it with a nasal cannula. Kathy shook her head. The double ended tube of the cannula fell away from her nostrils, but it was still close enough to provide her with the calming and system-feeding oxygen.

Dean stated a profound truth, "We need help. We can't do this on our own."

Rose crawled to the top of the hill then looked back. Kathy's chest was moving up and down in a calm and steady motion.

She smiled and gave herself a moment to feel, "Dean, bless your heart. And you didn't want to stop."

The second Rose popped her head over the hill she was blasted with questions, "Is she OK? Is she dead? Does she have any broken bones?"

After taking a self-preserving slow breath Rose straightened to an upright standing position and responded to the onlookers, "She is conscious, can feel her feet, there appears to be no spinal injuries, but her jaw is damaged. Has anyone called 911? We need the Jaws-of-Life to get her out of the car and an ambulance paramedic and EMT to assess her further and take her to the hospital. We've done all we can do."

A man stooped over his cell-phone pacing up and down the road responded, "I have a brand new cell-phone. I've been trying to get a signal. I don't really know how to use it, sorry."

"Please try again."

"I can't get a signal. Shit, I'm really sorry.

"Will someone, anyone please call 911? There are homes up the road. I need to stay here."

Rose glanced up the road. A light green Forest Service utility truck was approaching the scene. She ran to meet the driver halfway, "We can really use your help."

"How can I help?"

Rose told him what had happened and what they needed. He radioed dispatch, "Two car accident, one patient, EMT on-scene, needs Jaws, ambulance and CHP," followed by their location.

"Who needs the Jaws-of-Life?" dispatched responded.

"I'm an EMT with the Briggs Volunteer Fire Department. My partner, a first-responder, and I stopped to help. I was in the EMT class with the Digger fire department's chief and assistant-chief this spring. There's a woman in her late twenties or early thirties trapped in her car about ten yards down the ravine. She is conscious and alert. Her jaw is seriously damaged probably broken. She is C-collared and on fifteen liters of oxygen. She can feel her feet. No other injury is apparent. The car has been turned off. It appears to be stable."

The Forest Service officer spoke into his mike, "Copy that?"

"Dispatch copies."

The officer landed the palm of his right hand on the emergency brake of his truck then hedged, "Do you need me anymore? I got work to do. I've seen way too many of these."

Rose patted the lower edge of his window frame nodded with reassurance and said, "Thank you no."

He left. Rose didn't get his name. He brought stability and expertise at a crucial time to a situation in need. She was grateful.

Rose hurried back down the road and then announced, "The fire department and an ambulance are on their way."

From the top of the hill, Rose called out, "Dean, is Kathy still breathing, conscious and alert?"

"Yes, plus her jaw is in a more natural position. It's easier to understand her. She doesn't know what hit her. She's a lucky woman."

On the cliff-side of the road the truck driver was sitting next to his truck up against the wall on his haunches fingering the gravel. Rose let him be.

Chief Charles Hall of the neighboring Digger Fire Department arrived. Fire and Rescue equipped with the Jaws-of-Life pulled up shortly after, followed by the ambulance and the CHP. Fire and Rescue efficiently set out their equipment and proceeded to assess the situation. The CHP questioned the truck driver and measured the skid marks. The paramedic asked the truck driver if he felt he needed medical care. He shook his head. Then she climbed down the ravine and got out her stethoscope. Rose inhaled a shaky breath of guilt. She hadn't taken Kathy's blood pressure or checked her heart rate.

"Will she be OK?"

"Yes, she'll be OK. You guys did a good job."

Then Chief Charles Hall in a calm direct and respectful tone said, "May I take over the scene?"

"Yes, of course, but I don't understand why you're asking me that question."

"Rose, you got us here. That's what the Incident Commander does. Do you have any paperwork for me? I'll add it to my report."

She looked around and found the hardly used run-sheet under dirt, leaves and a tarp near their medical bag. She handed it to him, "It's not complete. I'll write-up a detailed report tonight and bring it in tomorrow."

"Thanks. She's lucky. You and your partner showed up at the right time."

Dean was replaced. He hauled himself up the hill and then cleaned the little blood that had splashed onto his hands. Rose retrieved the medical equipment from the ambulance EMT-driver to replenish what they had used, reorganized and closed the medical bag and lugged it back to the truck. They left the scene.

Once home they took long showers. Not so much as to wash the dirt and sweat of the accident from their bodies, but to wash the trauma away.

Stunned and needing confirmation, the minute Rose finished her shower she completed the report. Then well aware that it was paramount that she first established herself as a member of the Emergency Services, she called the hospital and identified herself in detail as a member of the Briggs Fire Department and her relationship with the said accident.

To the point, the attending physician declared, "Kathy needs extensive surgery from the complications brought on by the trauma to her jaw. Her injuries are limited to her jaw. Overall she is in good shape."

Emptied of the worry that she may have missed a vital piece of information, Rose allowed herself to lay the receiver into its cradle.

Months later Rose spoke to her paramedic friend Deidra, who had communicated with the paramedic at the accident. Evidently, she stuck around in the ER to witness the removal of the C-collar. She didn't believe the patient's jaw was broken. Dean had set her jaw and placed the C-collar that well. Rose was very proud. They saved a life.

Fires put the powers of fear and flight to the test.

"Wildland fire two miles NW of Stage Coach Road and River Lane." Screeching beepers and scanners blasted fear, anxiety and a rush of adrenaline into every member of the Briggs Volunteer Fire Department. It was August, a drought year, one Saturday late afternoon. The hot dry wind blew down from the north. A red-flag day, the potential for a fast moving, destructive wildland fire was at a peak.

Dean and Rose were members of the department for a little over a year. They dropped their chores, fed the animals and checked to be sure there was nothing left unsafe to harm their home and property. The fire was far enough away from their house so they believed it wouldn't devour their home. But they didn't bank on it. They closed up the house, airtight.

What Rose did, every move, every safety precaution was embedded in her from the months and months of trainings led by Chief Jim Brady. She could hear his words echo in her mind. Her innards quivered in anticipation of what she was about to experience.

Ready and waiting, their firefighting gear was stored in her VW Bug and Dean's truck. To protect them from the fire and be easily seen, they each donned blue jeans, a long sleeved cotton shirt layered over by a bright yellow Nomex shirt and pants, a cotton facemask and a fire resistant helmet. Goggles framed in thick black rubber covered their eyes. Leather high-top, lace-up, lugged-soled, steel-toed fire boots and wool socks insulated their feet. Leather gloves with forearm extensions completed their overall protective shield. Hooked onto to each of their belts were a folded fire-safe tent, a canteen of water and energy-bars. Only their names on the back of their helmets singled them out from all of the other firefighters.

They jumped into Dean's truck, pulled the emergency light-switch on and drove straight to Station 2. Their first indication that they were on the right track was the aroma of a freshly lit campfire. One tall plume of gray-brown smoke crept out of the distant pines to their north. They hopped into the old, trusty, 1974 Ford makeshift fire truck #1952. For over six month, they'd been assigned the responsibility of maintaining that fire truck. Both of them, on schedule, had checked its reliability. They believed in the power of their rig.

Rose summoned her inner calm. Then with an assurance in her role as a firefighter, strong and ready, she radioed dispatch, "Willow County Fire-1952 responding."

Dispatched confirmed, "Copy-1952 responding-wildland fire NW Stage Coach Road and River Lane."

Dean double-clutched the truck, to brake, to gas and back again, pushing the truck to its limits. Rose switched on the siren and beacon lights watching the ugly thick gray-brown plume of smoke widen. The fresh dry aroma of summer shifted acrid.

As they approached Stage Coach and River Lane the blinding dust hindered their vision and choked the air out of them. They fed into the multi-fire trucks that were descending into the thick tunnels of brush when the (CDF) spotter plane began giving directions to the responding fire-trucks. Over the radio, their number came up. There was no turning back. The pilot could see their skyward facing number painted on the cab. A helicopter with a water-filled bucket hung by a cable from its belly and an S-2 turbo prop aircraft filled with coral slush fire-retardant joined the battle from above.

Following the spotter plane's orders, Dean drove without reservation down the deeply rutted, brush encroached, dirt roads. When they reached a place to begin fighting the fire, Rose radioed dispatch, "Willow County Fire-1952 at scene."

Dispatch confirmed, "Copy-1952 at scene."

They couldn't tell exactly where they were. But they knew they were only a few acres away from life threatening, blazing heat, fire and smoke with thick layers of trees and brush between them. The wind was pushing oxygen-sucking smoke at them. They had to move fast or get the hell out of there.

"Damn, God give me strength." Rose thought, closing her eyes and dropping her chin to her chest.

The wind shifted, but there was no telling what it would do next. They parked in a spot that provided them with an escape route, with no immediate danger of approaching flames, but close enough to get to the fire. Rose flew out of the truck and shoved the chock block on the down side of a rear tire, securing the stability of the truck on a risky downward slope.

Leaving the truck's engine running in neutral and the emergency brake yanked tight, Dean jumped out of the driver's seat to face the pump's control panel on his side of the truck.

They looked straight into each other's eyes from opposite sides of the truck, dead serious. "I know you can do it," they thought. They were friends, comrades and firefighters.

From the back of the truck Rose yanked out the two hundred foot-long, 2 1/2 inch diameter, cotton fire hose, balanced the nozzle end on her right shoulder, gripped it tight with both hands and ran. The hose lay in organized layers to allow her to pull it out with no resistance. Weaving through trees and low brush, jumping, stepping then pushing herself over sharp rocks, periodically putting down the nozzle to run back and release the hose that hooked around a rock or low brush, she finally located a meadow just before the flames reached it.

Rose faced Dean and yelled, "Ready for water!" The fire was rapidly advancing towards her. The Turbo prop airplane rained down a long sweep of thick coral fire-retardant a few yards beyond the face of a forty foot wide wall of thick smoke and intense red-orange hot flames. The fire was eating up the bush that rose above her eye level. Pops sizzles, swirling wind and a continuous penetrating shrilling sound pierced her ears accelerating her already elevated heart rate. She stood straight and tall, in awe and fear twenty feet away from the blazing fire. "You could kill, but I won't let you."

Rose couldn't hear or see Dean, but she knew what he was doing, thinking and feeling. Again and again he tired to start the pump. But it wouldn't. "Shit! There's no way I'm about to tell Rose we're going to have to cut and run!" he cursed in frustration looking directly at the pump's control panel. But finally on the third or fourth try, a clinking sound reassured him that the pump was sure to start on the next try. He listened closely for the moment when the clinking sound told him to let go of the pump's starter switch. "NOW, I'm good to go." He throttled up the PSI level, listened to the pump's engine churn 500 gallons of water, opened the hose valve wide and then watched the water expand the hose. At the other ends, approximately one hundred and fifty feet away. Rose held the closed nozzle. He scanned the approaching path of the fire and yelled, "Water coming!!"

The oxygen-eating smoke and hot wind-driven fire was close, way too close to Rose. She began to back off, but then she heard Dean. To take in all that she could behind herself she twisted to the right and then focused her gaze down to the ground surveying the length of the flat waterless hose as it expanded and filled with surging water, all the way to the nozzle. She clutched the nozzle tight in her left hand and wrapped her right hand securely around the hose a foot up from the nozzle. With her body in a stable triangular stance, knees bent and planted into the ground, she inched the lever that opened the nozzle forward until it was wide-open then maneuvered the rotating end of the nozzle through its variations of streams to the correct one, full and straight. Without flinching, she shot the powerful stream of water at the ground level of the tallest flame twenty feet in front of her. Not stepping more than a few feet in any direction, Rose fanned the water from side to side, pushing the hot dirt and roots of the fire away from her.

The firewall dropped.

Rose made an about-face, focused on the flying ember-fed spot-fires that were creeping away from her only a couple of yards away and doused them with water. "Done! Our section is under control. We did it."

To preserve the valve and hose and not be the receiver of a back-lash that could whip her in the face and flatten her onto her back in seconds. With caution, Rose shut-off the nozzle. She let her arms fall to her side, lowered the nozzle to the ground and stood motion-less. She faced Dean who she knew was watching her progress and gave him a thumbs-up. He throttled down the PSI level.

Driven by adrenaline, will and training, it was only the length-ening of her shadow on the ground and hunger that gave her the notion that time had past.

The harsh smoke dissipated and the sky opened up to the sum-mer's bright blue. Rose located an unaffected spot in the meadow. She lowered her pelvis down onto the blistering dry grass, wrapped her arms around her knees, let her head drop between her legs and inhaled deep long breaths. Now, and only now, would she even consider removing her goggles and facemask.

A wash of coral slush fire-retardant clung to Rose's shoulders. Sweat poured down her red hot flushed face. Black soot covered her boots, gloves, yellow Nomex shirt and pants. She opened her canteen of water, drank its contents, poured some on her face, ate one of her energy-bars and then tried to relax.

It wasn't over yet, but Rose didn't want to move. She hurt like hell. Cramps snuck their way into her legs and arms, shaking and aching with fatigue.

But she ordered her entire being to, "Get-Up."

Rose exhaled out of the depths of her diaphragm. From a dis-tance she caught a glimpse of a helicopter dropping its' last bucket of water. The turbo prop airplane made one last sweep.

The ground crews were on-their-own now, amidst acres and acres of hot black coals, downed trees, and stumps embedded with smoldering fires. Water soaked brush gave off thick white steam. Blackened grass and stick-like trees surrounded the charred remains of out-buildings. Coral slush was splattered throughout this barren world. A smell akin to liquefied chicory root saturated the scorched wild land. Luckily, all the houses had been saved.

Rose and Dean joined the other firefighters from the Briggs Volunteer Fire Department and CDF, who were extinguishing their own sections of the fire, combining efforts to methodically douse the remaining hot embers. They connected Brass T's to the hose couplings every 200 feet and then attached one hundred foot long 1 1/2 inch hoses equipped with a smaller nozzle. The threat of flare-up was real. Short-cuts were not an option.

Rose slowly trampled through the hot barren post-fire world. Her leather high-top lug-soled boots allowed her to walk in places no other shoe could withstand. She felt no heat. Her gloved hands tugged the lighter nozzle and hose that extended down to the ground from her shoulder. The broiling sun beat down on her neck and back. She doused the smoldering embers, coals and tree stumps and then kicked over fallen trees. To discover red hot coals ready to start another fire when the world around it dried up once again. Tedious work, but with each simple task accomplished Rose released a bit of the built-up adrenaline that had affected every cell in her body.

The blazing sun was sinking into the horizon, Dean and Rose's animals 6pm feeding had come and gone. They disconnected and emptied the soot blackened hoses. They slung them onto their shoulders, hauled them back to #1952 and threw them on the truck-bed.

When they arrived at Station 2, bone-weary and hungry, Rose radioed dispatch, "Willow County Fire-1952 Station 2."

They scrubbed clean and hung up the wet hoses to dry and neatly replaced them with dry ready-to-use hoses.

Their eyes glazed over from exhaustion. They stopped and stared at each other. Covered with sweat, soot, fire-retardant and poison oak oil, Rose could barely speak. Nonetheless she said, "We did our part. It's time for us to go home, clean up, eat and get on with life."

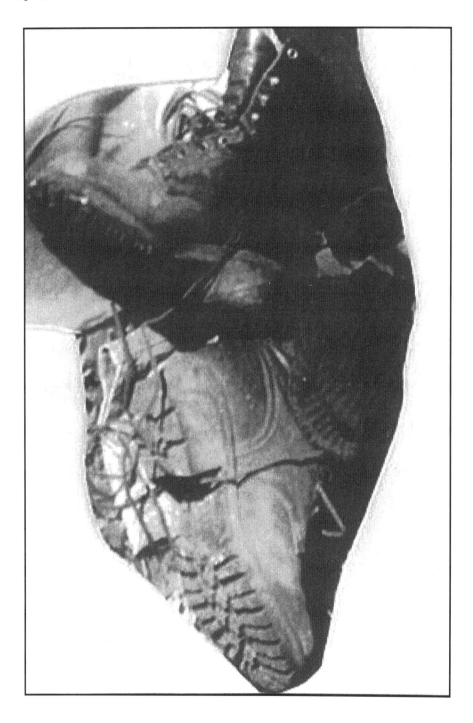

Good and evil are equally supported by nature.
R.L. Wing

Two years into the fire department Rose witnessed the removal of her chief, Jim Brady. Faced with the corrupt power-hungry members of the department, he fought for the respect he rightfully deserved. He requested that anyone who supported him as chief, to please come to the board meetings and voice their feelings. She was a major part of the workings of the department, but not the administration. She didn't know what he was up against. She had absolutely no experience in political gamesmanship. In time, what she knew of it through gossip-driven personal she saw as unworthy of her, an honest and forthright person. She wished him well and promised to continue to be a reliable responding member of the department.

Rose went about learning the truth, but at the same time disbelieving it. She regretted not saying and ultimately doing more. Fire Chief Jim Brady and six experienced, loyal captains and firefighters/EMT left the Briggs Volunteer Fire Department. They were all her mentors. As soon as a call came over her beeper a terrible dread came over her. They wouldn't be there. Rose was torn, leave or stay to complete her calling.

Dean had made it clear that he wasn't drawn to be a public servant. He offered words of empathy and warnings of excessive involvement, but never gave her an ultimatum. Rose's dedication to the department put a wedge between them. Their priorities weren't opposite, but were no longer parallel.

For the following two years Rose was the top responding non-officer. Because no one can accomplish all that is asked of emergency medical service personnel on their own, she never lost sight of one first-responder who came forth and stabilized calls with his dedication, reliability and consistency like no other.

The old and new chief had requested that all responding officers and firefighters partner up when and if possible. The amount of personal vehicles on scene needed to be reduced. Kevin lived one mile from Station 1. The rescue rig and other emergency vehicles were housed there. He was frequently available, a long-time resident of their small town and one of the first dispatchers for the department before the 911 emergency service existed in their community. As a teenager, Kevin's mother was the manager of the only market in town. She'd pick up the phone at the market then relay the emergency to her son. Kevin instigated the phone chain that got the fire department up and moving.

Kevin knew Rose would be at a call if she could, knew where she lived and figured out her direction of travel in her personal vehicle. They met up at a corner or on the road. She parked, locked her car and hopped in.

Kevin was a first-responder, a rank below Rose. He made her aware of it when necessary. He needed an answer, an order and to show respect for her amongst the other members of the department. She never used his rank to lesson his importance to his face or otherwise. She depended on his cool head and attention to her needs as the patient-care giver. He was the recorder; responsible for taking down the vital information that Rose acquired. He retrieved any equipment she needed from the rescue-rig, gathered information from witnesses, loved ones and fellow Briggs Volunteer Fire Department personnel. Then to complete his role he gave the arriving paramedics the present state of the patient or patients. With Kevin, Rose didn't have to think twice. Consequently, she could focus on the patients' needs and not have to hold on to the information as it changed and multiplied. Without him her work as an EMT-D would have slipped into chaos. There was no one that could match Kevin's professionalism at a medical call.

It's hard to leave any deeply rooted life style,
even if it's destroying you.

The second and final year Rose was the top responding non-officer thrust her into seriously questioning the political climate of the department.

She had responded to over five hundred 911 medical related calls plus fifteen wildland fires. Some were short lived, some long, some with Dean, others included her working side-by-side with CDF firefighters. She was in vital roles, in the center of the bull's eye, vulnerable, both physically and mentally to the ever present post traumatic effects of emergency calls.

In addition, Rose assisted a neighboring elderly couple. She and Dean knew Chuck and Ethel long before the drinking, smoking and poor eating habits set the stage for their inevitable demise. Unbeknownst to Rose, her emotional attachment to them was contributing to the process of her own potential early decline.

The couple lived a two minute walk down the road. Ethel suffered from emphysema and congestive heart failure. A devoted woman, she drove her husband Chuck, suffering from kidney failure, the thirty miles to his weekly dialysis treatments.

Rose wasn't at liberty to diagnose, but the signs were written all over them. She knew in her gut that it was only a matter of time before they'd die. She hoped Ethel would allow Chuck his wish to stop the treatment and let nature takes its course.

Rose never said a word. It was not her place. Who died first she doesn't remember. She left the department before their demise, but in the interim she lacked the boundaries she desperately needed. She was caught-up in who she perceived herself to be. The EMT that would do what was needed 24/7.

After too many 911 calls that alerted people far beyond her and in the end weren't necessary, Rose suggested that all those living near the couple offer their personal phone numbers. Most did. She welcomed the responsibility, but as time went by, Chuck and Ethel assumed that she would come to their aid.

Rose reset the oxygen tank, opened the windows to let the readily available oxygen from the great outdoors in and picked Chuck up from the floor when he fell out of his chair or bed. Ethel, obese and periodically emotionally unavailable, couldn't or wouldn't.

Fire department personnel members, who lived close-by, were alerted by the couple. To Rose's dismay, the kiss of death Heath Mat frequently passed the task to Rose. It didn't always work out to the benefit of her or the patient.

On the run Rose called Heath's home, "Heath, Chuck needs to be picked up and put back onto his bed. It's hard on my back. I need your help."

Heath arrived, his father in tow. Heath assumed Rose wanted him to radio dispatch for an ambulance. Frustrated and bewildered she struggled to, once again, explain her needs.

Stern and put-upon, he preceded to pick Chuck up off the floor and hoist him onto his bed. Chuck thanked Heath profusely.

It was not until Ethel said, "Rose arrived here first. She's the one we've been counting on for months. Chuck, thank her," did the respect and admiration Chuck bestowed to Heath come Rose's way.

Rose accepted the facts. Chuck was weak and pale or black and blue throughout his entire body. It was a wonder he recognized anyone.

Not long after the disheartening incident when the phone rang her entire body went stiff. Consequently, she chose to monitor personal and 911 calls with a fierce scrutiny. There was no way she was going to talk to or do for anyone unless she wanted to. It was time to take a real good look at her life.

Rose was trained to perform CPR out in the field, was a certified instructor and understood the idea of it. But when she had to perform CPR on a patient she was fully aware that it only worked 2% of the time.

For up to thirty minutes, Rose proceeded to administer CPR with the help of fellow members of the department. They kept going. It was their duty. The paramedics had to arrive and call it, "Dead, Stop," before they could stop. The stench from the released bodily fluids made her gag. Her innards were ready to throw-up, but her intestines were too tight and squeezed dry. In the mist of chest compressions and breaths she was well aware that it provided only a false hope. To her, it was demeaning to the patient, the witnessing loved ones and the EMS personnel. They couldn't save a high percentage of lives with this procedure. It was an illusion hammered into their minds, the belief that they could bring a patient back to a functioning productive life after they went into cardiac arrest.

What Rose witnessed as an EMT is under the laws of patient confidentially. This fact separates EMTs from the majority of the population. As an EMT in a very small town, a town with lovers of gossip and a willingness to expand on any truth, she had to put up a wall to protect the integrity that she held dear.

Numerous times Rose was forced to politely say, "I can't tell you anything. Patient confidentially is a law I as an EMT must abide by," to one particular woman.

Sally, an employee of Brigg's bustling grocery store, for reasons Rose was unable to comprehend, gnawed at her. Often, she had only a minor piece of information, but that was all it took to spark her curiosity and attempt to sift personal information of the sick and injured out of her. Sally's lack of sensitivity sickened Rose. Well aware that Kevin's mother, the manager would fire Sally on the spot if she knew her lack of integrity tightened Rose's resolve.

Sally did stop, but not until one afternoon only hours after a particularly difficult call.

Enraged by this woman's corrupt mind, Rose exploded. She took hold of her fury and then in a low even tone said, "Sally, try to imagine if you had to call 911 for yourself or a loved one. Would you want the whole community to know about it? I doubt it. Think about that the next time your curiosity gets the better of you."

Sally appeared to understand.

Sally was not alone. To some members of the EMS inner circle, knowing the private lives of patients strengthened their ego.
It saddened Rose to witness the insensitivity of humanity. They
were trained to assist the sick and injured not feed on it. She and
the few colleagues she respected continued to hold on to their professionalism, nonetheless. If they hadn't Rose would have left the
emergency services long before she did.

Outside the fire department's immediate environment Rose
received personal recognition. The words, looks of gratitude and
overall appreciation from the community were heartwarming. On
the other side of the coin, suspicion lingered in the minds of a
few patients and their loved ones. They suspected that Rose had
seen, and most likely did, something the patient and their family wanted to hide. Some didn't believe she could keep it to herself. She did, even when questioned by gossip-driven community
members. Rose carried a deep respect for personal privacy and
attempted to convey that to any and all who needed the reassurance. It was in her bones.

Rose's self-assurance had strengthened with each call. She
was proud of herself, but she was a target. After four years of being
equally ranked, but rarely working side-by-side with Heath Mat
as a firefighter/EMT-D and CPR instructor she was a threat to
the now Captain Heath Mat. Seething with jealousy, he and those
under his spell put little holes in her efforts. Actions and words
unknown to her, except deep inside her subconscious, were spoken
by him to brainwash the unsuspecting new and easily manipulated members of the department against her. She was devastated
and disheartened beyond comprehension when all that she knew
from years of experience was disregarded. In time it destroyed
her confidence and the status that she had attained with integrity,
will and compassion.

Rose lost much of the long-standing community support. A devoted firefighter/EMT-D Rose could hardly believe what was happening to her. Captain Heath Mat withered her soul with no outburst of violence. There was nothing she could do but accept that she had lost, for the time being, to a power-hungry male-chauvinist experienced in the ways of corruption.

One can only understand people if you feel them in yourself. Rose was a professional. The fact that good and evil are supported by nature equally was not a part of her understanding yet.

Right has nothing to do with the real world. Heath Mat was a man who thought too well of himself. People gravitate toward those who exude a powerful charisma. He was such a man. It was not simply because Rose was a woman. It did come into play, but it was more the fact that she had the ability to make decisions without his direction or approval. Moreover, those who are limited in their position, a team player, lose their identity. Rose was not about to do that for any organization or person.

Honesty is a rare commodity.

Perhaps negative emotions are the most powerful screen
of denial that sits before us or washes over us.
J. Douglas Mitchell D.C.

Fatigue crept into Rose's unsuspecting pores. She was losing connection to the realities that she held onto for a decade. On top of everything else that was happening in the fire department she was living alone after an alarming finale with her partner, Dean. She had her horse, dog, and three cats to care for on five acres in the house he and she had built nine years ago. After a long battle, a fight she didn't want to be a part of but it was impossible. It was a matter of survival not only for herself but to raise her furry friends in a loving environment. Her insistence that the property be bought as two unmarried individuals kept her out of the courtroom. Rose owned her half of the property outright.

Dean lived on the, once owned by them, parcel next door. He paraded his new girlfriend right in front of her. She could hear them having sex. Why he needed to do that Rose never found out. It was, in her eyes, immature and completely unnecessary. She and Dean were over.

Jobs she loved became impossible to fulfill. She couldn't concentrate. She wanted to hide from anyone who she feared might need her.

Nonetheless, Rose had a hard time letting go of the belief that the six and a half year identity and commitment to her local volunteer fire department ended in a sea of political maneuvers. As a strong-minded, experienced and respected member of the community, during her professional career as a firefighter/EMT-D, she received recognition from the paramedics as they arrived to load up the patients into the ambulance on its way to the hospital. CDF captains allowed her to work directly with their firefighters extinguishing fires. She was the trusted firefighter's association treasurer for five years. Because of her top responding non-officer status she was publicly honored as the Firefighter of the Year once.

But the next year, Captain Heath Mat, with his sights on becoming chief and an underlying throbbing jealousy for strong-minded self-reliant people, changed the objective criteria for the honor of having one's name on the plaque with those who came before you as Firefighter of the Year. A popular vote among the members of the department was accepted by Chief Bud Taurus and his officers at an officer's meeting dominated by Captain Heath Mat.

Objectivity lost, Rose publicly received a certificate stating she was the top responding non-officer not Firefighter of the Year. It was the first of many behind-the-scene maneuvers that she was aware of.

"It's not the critic who counts, not the man who points out how the strong man stumbled or where the doer of good deeds could have done better.

The credit belongs to the man who is actually in the arena, whose face is marred by dust and sweat and blood, who strives valiantly, who errs and comes up short again and again, who knows the great enthusiasms, the great devotions and spends himself in a worthy cause, who at his best knows in the end the triumph of high achievement and who at the worst, if he fails, at least fails while daring greatly, so that his place shall never be with those cold and timid souls who know neither victory or defeat."

Teddy Roosevelt-26th President of the United States of America

Rose returned every piece of fire department issued property. She was forty-seven years old, athletic and beautiful. Briggs Volunteer Fire Department and the EMS service personnel outside the district were her family.

She was informed. At the following training, a self-serving determination to build a foundation for his political future wrapped in his habitual fake exterior of gratitude, cold and satisfied, the now Chief Heath Mat stated, "Rose has returned her gear. A dedicated member of the department for many years she is experiencing burn out."

Rose's identity was pulled out from under her. Blindsided when she believed in herself in a most profound way brought great sorrow to her life.

It wasn't until five years later that ex-members of the department came forth with more truths of Heath Mat's devious ways to undermine Rose's professionalism and empathy.

Part Six

Years of "marriage" hadn't made me less curious.

The freshly sprouted oak leaves began their arduous opening into the comforting tepid air. Meadow grasses, shooting stars, wild irises, buttercups and Rose's dearly beloved crocuses had popped their heads above ground. Time for a new beginning. Two years broken apart from Dean after twelve years together. Though he lived nearby, Rose's heart was raw and not available to that man.

She caught glimpses of Russell in the local café, across from Ruby's Glad Rags, her place of employment. When he cruised through the streets of Briggs she couldn't take her eyes off of him. Everything about him drew her into her need to feel. She'd never seen a more alluring man. Slender build, not more than an inch or two taller than her, chiseled weather-beaten face, penetrating blue-green eyes, tight Levis, an earth toned tee-shirt and rugged work boots.

Rose couldn't help but wonder if he noticed her. She made a conscious yet elusive focus to acquire the ways of the well-put-together man's life, but only knew his name because others had said it. It was her style to watch and listen first.

Then one mild spring day, she was in the shop. Russell was eyeing a display of earrings. Rose was straightening up at the far end of the counter when he said his first words to her, "Can you help me find a gift?" that swung open the door, but only a crack.

Rose slid closer.

He lowered his gaze, tucked his hands into his jean pockets then whispered, "What do you like?"

Rose picked out and then placed a couple pairs of earrings on the counter that she hoped to buy for herself. It was an everyday occurrence for men to ask her, the salesgirl, what to buy for their sister, girlfriend or wife, but what a lovely man. His response, delicate, at ease and polished melted a part of her heart that she'd forgotten.

Out of the blue from the other side of the store, Betty yelled, "Rose, I need help," odd behavior for her upbeat exuberant colleague.

Puzzled, Rose excused herself.

As soon as Russell was out of sight a wide-eyed Betty vigorously waved Rose to come near. In a hush she said, "He's been coming in a lot. He looks around, seemingly for someone, than leaves. You are the first salesgirl he has spoken to. He's stalking you. Be careful."

Rose turned around. He was gone.

Call a stop. Close the door. Be safe.

But his interest lifted Rose. She was floating about. Russell's comings and goings in and out of the café directly across the street became a focus. Dean had shown little value in her long before their separation. At the café Russell greeted her as she swished by. Periodically he invited her to sit at his table. The short and sweet inquisitive conversations aroused her. But outside its walls he disregarded her existence. The paradox was unrelenting. She wanted him, but why put her heart-on-her-sleeve and subject herself to the ups and downs of love once again.

In her loneliness she fantasized. Little bits of attention became a priority. They carried her far.

Dean was living next door in a house he had built without the regard to Rose's equal ownership of the property it sat on. It was not for him to build anything on it without her OK. She was as legally responsible for it as him, but he didn't see it that way. Moreover he found a new mate that appeared to nurture him in ways Rose had left behind on her quest to be whole.

Dean and Rose had divided their property, but no fence had been built to physically mark the boundaries. Her horse Lana deserved a pasture to extend her life and to run as free as the boundaries of the fence allowed. Rose wanted to do this for her dear horse.

A year after Rose's first sighting of Russell. One sweet smelling cool morning in the delightful month of May, they sat at opposite ends of the café counter. She overheard him say to all who were listening, "I'm looking for work."

Rose hopped out of her chair and shimmed herself into the empty stool right next to him and then with enthusiasm but not so assertive as to frighten him away she inquired, "Do you do fencing?"

Shy, but nonetheless open to her he responded, "No, I leave that up to the younger men."

But this was her chance. How many others would she get? He could help her and she wanted to know this man. With desire hidden deep inside her words she came out with a plea, "You can do it. I'll help."

Sunrise the next day, Russell came by. They walked the property line and determined what materials were needed to build the fence. Rose called Home and Garden Fencing and received a quote, wrote a check made out to them then handed it to Russell.

He returned shortly.

After all the materials to build the fences were out of Russell's truck they placed them along the property line.

Dean, a powerful man, was watching every move they made. Rose was doing something she'd wanted to do for Lana long before they parted, but he never agreed.

Rose had called the building department, asked where the correct position the fence should be built in relationship to the line. They said, "Right on it."

She had support. It gave her the power. She needed to protect her shattered heart.

Determined to do what was right for her horse, but moreover for herself, she made her way to Dean. Three yards from the property line, just outside his workshop and home he stood rigid, arms crossed and scowling.

Faking a calm professionalism that hid her shaky nerves she stated, "I called the building department yesterday. I told them exactly what kind of fence I intended to build. They said building the fence on the property line was the correct position."

Dean was fuming. He took two measured steps toward Rose bore his fists into his hips, pressed his lips together and sent poison daggers from his eyes directly into her chest. He stated, "Its two feet to each side of the property line that ALL fences are SUPPOSED to be built."

Rose repeated herself only because she felt she had to. Then she resigned herself to the fact that Dean and she would never come to a peaceful end. She stepped away, back to her life.

Over her well-worn coveralls she tied a grass stained gardener's tote bag around her waist and then filled the pouches full of fencing post clips and the fence pliers.

Posthole digger in hand, Russell dug the holes for the treated poles and then pounded the metal poles into the ground, ten feet apart. The ground had absorbed the winter's rain easing his way.

Rose mixed the cement in her wheelbarrow and then filled the gaps that surrounded the treated poles after they set them into the holes.

Russell unrolled the barbless wire, pulled it taught and held it in place. The moon shaped sharp end of the fence pliers enabled Rose to catch one side of the fencing post clips and bend it so it connected the wire to the metal poles.

Together they systematically fastened each wire to pole connection one at a time. Their eyes met, their hands touched and the motion of them found a way to express how they felt for each other.

When the fencing pliers hook went into the eye of the fence post clips Rose felt an acute sense of need wafting between Russell and her. Slow sensual throbs deep inside her crotch sent moisture down her inner thighs. She wanted this job, this feeling to go on and on and on.

A dreadful forbidden reticence descended on them the moment that she hammered the last fencing nail into the final pole. Standing at the end of the long freshly built fence, they straightened up and then looked into each other's eyes. What Rose couldn't say Russell did, soft and wanting, "I wish this job wasn't over, I will miss you."

Deeply, passionately, Rose felt the same, but the emotional and physical energy it took to complete the separation of land between Dean and her was exhausting.

Stepping back to give herself some breathing room, hoping to convey her gratitude, keep her integrity and acknowledge the fact that Dean was not far away she said, "Russell, what do I owe you? If it wasn't for you this may not have ever happened."

His shinning eyes met hers, he swallowed, lifted his hand to her shoulder and then with an unknown tenderness touched it, "Nothing Rose... Before I leave I need you to know that I wasn't stalking you. It may have appeared that way, but I wasn't. I was getting up the nerve to talk to you."

Rose smiled. She understood. Side-by-side too afraid to touch, Russell and Rose sauntered over to Lana's paddock. Rose offered him the pleasure of releasing her to a new way of life. The moment Russell swung open the gate Lana flew by. Pleasure and joy filled Rose's inner feelings.

They loaded up his truck and then said their goodbyes. Rose's gaze followed the truck down the road. She turned to survey their creation, the fence, with hope for better days.

There was no turning back. The line was drawn.

In the gentleness of the evening's breeze, Rose was winding down, tired. The phone rang. It was him, "I miss you. Call me if you have other things you need done," a voice, a longing voice, Russell's voice.

In kind she responded, "I miss you too. Thanks so much for all your help. I will let you know, I promise."

Rose had more work for Russell. He allowed her to pay him. He used his weed-eater to cut her overgrown grass and delivered hay and materials for a vegetable garden.

Her previous love had failed her, spoke ill of her and let her secrets flow from his mouth. She needed a man of silence. Rose found him in Russell.

Russell said, "You'll be disappointed," pulling away from her hug of thanks after his work was done, but their chemistry said otherwise.

Rose could hear his truck coming a half mile away. She shivered in delight when she saw him. Her entire body was waiting for him.

That was the spring to winter of Rose and Russell. They explored each other's bodies too long untouched, previously injured and assumed by others. Years of unexpressed passion flowed through her hands onto his welcoming body.

Giggle induced water fights landed them on the soaked leaves and dirt and then rocked their bodies in laughter, hugs and kisses.

In the kitchen, Russell washed the dishes after a meal. Rose moved in. She couldn't, she didn't what to stop herself. She clung to his back. He stopped for her. Bubbles of soap from his hands dripped down her shorts and thighs. Turning to face her, he caressed her with a thoughtfulness unfelt by her until then. He laid the palm of his hands on her cheeks, wet her lips with his tongue and lifted her onto the kitchen counter. Then he took his time to find passion's edge and never stopped loving her until passion's needs had been met.

They rose to the heavens curled around each other in her hammock. On air, Rose followed Russell to her house. She invited him to sit on her porch swing. They were content to simply feel the warmth of each other close by as they watched the sun fall behind the trees. She stood. It was time for him to go. He brought his hands to his face, her scent was lingering. They waved their goodbyes.

Then he called that night to say, "I didn't wash my hands until long after I got home."

A few days later, sleeping on her living room floor only after kisses altered their consciousness. Rose awoke to a lovely creature beside her, warm and untroubled, snoring. He opened his eyes to her touch, "How'd you sleep?"

"Like a rock. Your floor is as hard as any, but with you near it calms my soul. Hate to go, but I need to get home. My son calls in the evenings. He's having personal problems."

Rose, void of the experience of having children, felt a little lost for words, but she knew personal problems well. "Sorry to hear that. See you later."

"You will."

Then there was that sultry late afternoon when Russell was covered with dust and silky succulent grass. Tuckered out they sat on her steps just outside the front door resting in silence for some time. The smell of earth, sweat and newly cut pasture sent fiery juices through Rose's groin. He, with a little request from her, was about to go inside to shower alone, but his eyes said, "Come along."

Within the space of time that he took to shift his weight, Rose mustered up the nerve to say, "Let me know when you're ready for me."

In a soft whisper, almost impossible to hear Russell said, "Now."

They entered the shower's fine mist. He was as into the moment as she. Bodies moved in a rhythm of their own design, their touch, sliding soap suds and wet slippery skin. Behind him, his curly dark brown hair speckled with flecks of gray that encircled his ears and fell to his temples mesmerized all that she was at that moment. Her fingers wrapped around his skull. She kneaded his head, face and neck. With a long continuous stroke her palms and long fingers embraced the contours of his lean, muscular torso gliding down to his buttocks, circling to his pelvic belly. He turned around. As her arms and leg wrapped around him, she melted into his very being and he slipped himself into her. His eye lids closed in passion's pleasure and then he inhaled a deep breath to exhale a long groan, "Rose." Engulfed in passions womb they embraced and undulated until the cloud of desire lifted, utterly saturated.

His essence remained long after he left her sofa. For the rest of the day, Rose soaked in the nest of him covered only by the towel they'd shared to dry off. Her heart danced.

They continued to come together for a while and trust each other with their secrets.

When death threatened to swallow the rest of her life Russell's deep voice resonated in her breath of life, "Don't give up," giving her hope within the hopelessness of being cut off from support, isolated and without the assurance of her once propelling position within the community she loved.

> *We opened each other's hearts, but our paths, our*
> *Truths needed us in other places besides*
> *In each other's arms.*

If you ask me if I believe in God I am forced to answer
does God believe in us.

Matt Cohen

EMS personnel "never" went into therapy. If someone did it was
kept secret. It's considered "a sign of instability."

Rose was a person she hardly recognized. Her drooping eyelids
were framed with the shallow red circles of fatigue. Her once
slim muscular physique was holding excess weight loose and dry.
Anxiety rang in her ears and stinging hot nerve pain trapped her
within an imaginary water clock. Sleep evaded her. Gray clouds of
despair surrounded her every move. Fear's loneliness fell upon her.

Her mental function went haywire. She put herself into a tall
tree forest of enemies. Chief Heath Mat and his willing pawns
invaded into her head. She had worn a gator's skin to work in
the emergency world. It was peeling away. The faces, numbers
and details of emergency scenes long past turned into ongoing
nightmares.

*In the pitch black darkness of a moonless night, I sped down the
unlit and deserted highway in my car with my emergency lights
on. I was in pursuit of three fire and rescue trucks. They had
opened up their piercing sirens, lights flashed, red, red, red, red,
red, on, off, on, off. They came to an abrupt halt.*

*I flew out of my car. EMT medical bag in hand, I knelt down
next to a known character on the side of the road. I was well
aware that this belligerent, filthy man had a history. He misused
any drug he could get his hands on. He was what the EMS world
in the privacy of their minds, the fire station and their homes
called a "frequent flyer."*

*I ripped open the zipper and grabbed the oxygen tank and
non-breather mask. I made every attempt to place the mask
over the airway of the alcohol and urine saturated cigarette and
marijuana smelling, dirty-mouthed, thrashing hitch-hiker. He
was about to pass out. It was all I could do to not wish it. But*

if he did I'd have to touch him. Shake him conscious, talk false reassuring words to keep him awake. God forbid do CPR.

Massive in both size and persona Chief Heath Mat loomed over me. His cold-blooded critical eyes examined every move I made. In a flash, he left me tending to my patient. Long stiff disjointed strides took him back and forth from one end of the emergency to the other. He stomped in my direction. Came to a stand still right above me and demanded, "What's his pulse rate? What's his blood pressure? I want that information now. What is it?"

On autopilot, obedient and duty bound I responded, "Yes, sir."

A caustic man when provoked or challenged, he drove the order into my lower back, "Now, DO it, now or he will DIE. It's YOUR responsibility!"

I lifted my gaze and then made an appeal, "I need help," to Chief Heath Mat's elusive professionalism.

From the corner of my eye I saw Bret, a tall, lanky blond, newly ranked first-responder approaching. He was one of the "good old boys". I felt his detachment. He was just going through the moves awaiting his deliverance. Surrounded with an air of absolutely no intention of assisting if at all possible, he stood erect directly over me then let out, "Can I help?"

Pulling up my professionalism from the depths of who I knew I was, I tried to control myself but failed. I pleaded, "Please help me, take his blood pressure."

Bret didn't move. He avoided eye contact. Ice cold he responded, "If you don't really need me, I have to go back to work," followed by an elaborate explanation of what his immediate work project at home entailed.

In full view of not only Bret, but Chief Heath Mat, an abusive forbidding man that I must obey or lose my right to assist patients, I went rigid. I gave in. Weak and meek I sighed, "Fine, Go."

Bret and the chief strolled away. They made small talk. Bret received a nod from the chief acknowledging his presence at the call and left.

Chief Heath Mat and his herd were near. They were always near. I couldn't help but glare at the gang of would-be officers. Bewildered and unable to comprehend who they thought they were completely removed from the dirty, emotional and life threatening work. They wanted, needed to be a member of the chief's favorites, receive some small token gesture that made them feel that they belonged to him. It made me want to puke. His army was nuzzling up in admiration of the mere fact that he could talk on the radio and order others around. Those orders I knew he couldn't fulfill. He had never been able to fulfill.

Chief Heath Mat smirked in relish of the importance bestowed upon him, separate from the norm radio in hand, seeking the public prestige and limelight.

It was not who I was. I was like the other members of the department devoted to the work, rushing to get the job done.

A flash of truth hastened the dissolution of my once zest for life. I was being abused. My talent, my know-how, all that I had studied so hard to learn was not in the least bit appreciated by that man. I was a threat to be eliminated.

Exposed to the manipulations of man, my breath was shallow and rapid, my pores oozed out high voltage adrenaline, my jaw clutched with pain.

Then the world behind my eyes drifted into a fluid distorted blur. I went into slow motion. I felt the bed under my body. A light and slippery cover protecting me from the cold night lay upon my fragmented spirit.

Rapid shifting visions of rushing flashing red lights, piercing sirens, the stench of burning rubber and dead bodies made my mind gyrate. Brown nosed emergency service personnel shifted my kind frame of mind to anger. It forced me to look at my existence. Those feelings I'd stuffed inside to fulfill a public servant's ideal. Caught in the middle of my subconscious and conscious I longed for the vision that might present itself outside my mind's eye.

Rose forced her eyes open. In an instant, the readily available solace, her bubble of hibernation, appeared. It was her room decorated in the delicate and soothing pictures and colors of nature.

Wish as she did, Rose couldn't lay in her paradise of peace for long. She needed to eat, care for her animals and keep her home and property in order. She wanted to simply enjoy her days free of the evil side of the Briggs Volunteer Fire Department.

Rose got up, dressed and then asked herself. "Who do I trust enough to understand and accept my situation?"

She had helped so many people at a moment's notice. Surely they would help her.

Disbelief preceded the friends that came through. The myth of Rose, courageous and driven, distorted her needs. In time, she came to understand that the majority of the community saw her as a fallen, high profile member of the very small community and were too busy to care. They assumed she'd be there for them. Not the other way around.

Rose turned to the medical world, but she was apprehensive of what she might encounter. She had quietly, but it got around, questioned the use and value of prescribed drugs. An action not supported by the medical model.

Rose's blood work came back normal, except for out of balance hormones. A medical health care professional diagnosed her with the immune system disorder fibromyalgia and post-traumatic stress syndrome. She couldn't make sense of it. Her life didn't make sense.

She began hormone therapy, but only after much inner struggle did Rose succumb to a regimen of high doses of the strongest form of anti-depressant, anxiety-relief drug available. The medical world provided her with a list of counselors in the area. No recommendations, no words of advice, nothing. Not one word was mentioned about the body-mind altering effects of diet and lifestyle.

Flabbergasted, Rose said, "How about if I change my diet? Could that help?"

A short heavyset nurse in his fifties furrowed his brows and shook his head. With the self-satisfaction of a know-it-all declared, "It's not our job," then stomped away.

List in hand, Rose ventured out to care for herself in the best way she knew how. But she was lost and frightened. Rose wanted to, tried to run as fast as she could from the changes that came over her.

To her long time General Practitioner she screamed, "I want my body back," to no avail.

His response, "Menopause is a part of the aging process," was perplexing. It was as if her body was revolting. She depended on, believed in her body for her identity and purpose in life. Others had come first for years. Her true self was hidden in the recess of a life. A life left behind long ago.

A dense fog hung between Rose and the rest of the world. Overwhelmed by the memories of 911 calls and the betrayal of Chief Heath Mat and his army, Rose went into her inner world. A world she hardly knew.

For one solid year the side effects of the anti-depressant moved Rose's thoughts. It dulled her mind and blurred her vision. Paranoia set in.

She stopped being able to even look at her car Sammy, as anything but an emergency vehicle. She sat in the driver's seat, hoped to drive herself the few miles to the grocery, gas station or bus stop. But when seconds turned into minutes the simple act of sitting behind the steering wheel severe heart palpations, sweats and uncontrollable shakes inhabited her spirit. Even so, she started the car. She moved it a little. She let it run without her in it. She wasn't going to give up Sammy.

The removal of that particular anti-depressant by the FDA was unbeknownst to Rose until a year after she on her own, bit by bit, paying very close attention to her moods, weaned herself off of it. Periodically she discussed her situation with an MD or a counselor, but it was she who willed herself free of it.

Rose had to truly believe and not stop believing that her needs came first.

As an infant, Rose was baptized a Quaker. Her mother held her one and only baby girl in front of the elders of the church and promised to bring Rose up the Quaker way. She was a birthright Quaker.

Quakers believe that God is within each and every one of us. It was a battle to believe that truth. "Where is he?" Rose asked herself, "What does he want from me? Am I one of God's children? Do I deserve to be one of God's children?"

Rose was sickened by the thought of having the blood of her parents flowing through her veins, but to be God's child resonated warmth and a belonging within her divine essence.

Laura, a counselor Rose came to appreciate, asked her when they were about to sit down at a table with four chairs, "Where would you like to sit?"

Rose politely responded, "Wherever you'd like."

Laura stated without emotion or judgment, "Rose you need to say where you want to sit. That's what you're here for."

Rose fingered one chair and then quietly said, "Here."

The first step to Rose's recovery was set in motion.

Rose made calls for help. She was eternally grateful to her old friends who agreed. But when the manager of the caregivers in the area arrived at her home it took all Rose had not to lose her dignity. She was handed the appropriate forms and a list of chores to be performed by a housekeeper twice a week. The manager investigated the safety of Rose's home. The throw rugs that Rose had placed ten years ago had to go. "You may slip and fall, break a bone and have to call 911."

That women's explicit and poignant words weakened Rose's very being.

Rose could only shuffle within the six hundred square foot space that she inhabited. Her beloved sun filled loft was now a distant memory. Her efforts to bathe were compounded by the fact that she couldn't stand long enough to shower, but she wouldn't check yes on the line that asked, "Do you need personal bathing assistance?"

The following day, Alice, a woman in her thirties was sent to Rose's home. Lying in her bed downstairs, Rose was intensely aware of Alice's approach into her space. She knocked then hesitated. It was only after Rose weakly responded, "Come in," that she entered. Then she sweetly asked Rose how she was doing and didn't seem to mind that she had little to say. Alice showed her the food that she had bought from Rose's specifications then proceeded to prepare multiple meals for the days between her visits. While Alice tidied up they exchanged stories.

Alice was a courteous and accommodating person. Her food preparation was nurturing and informative. Rose was comforted by her, but after only a few months Alice's personal life took her out of the area. Rose missed her a great deal. She made a point to call the agency and ask for her return with no luck.

The agency sent another housekeeper and another.

Watching the light and shadows come and go throughout the days was Rose's work, her journey and purpose. After all the phone calls were made, her friends who visited far too infrequently left or the housekeeper hadn't yet arrived or was gone for the day, the faces within the trees expressed what Rose felt, lost and alone.

The changing shapes of the shadows took on a life of their own. Rose absorbed the images, dark and dismal or bright and warming. It was what she had to fill her day, to breathe into her existence beyond the weakness, pain, hot flashes, sweats and the exhaustion of her life force. There was a peace and quiet unlike anything she had ever experienced seeping into her being.

A single step took great effort. Strain Rose had never known. A spot in the depths of Rose's core, that she could feel when her focus was nowhere else, held the key to her survival. An imaginary tiny and very dim single candlelight's flicker lived in the cave of her solar plexus. It fed the flame of her desire to live. To die would fulfill a need inside those whom she didn't respect. She once had joy in her life. She once had authority over herself. Rose held on to those thoughts, moment after moment, even when the only move-ments she took were when she willed herself into the kitchen to heat up a prepared meal, eat it at the kitchen table, go to the bath-room and then go back to bed.

One afternoon the drizzling rains of fall kept me company. As I fell asleep to the sound of the running water coming from my cassette player my essences lifted. It floated above, stood look-ing at my body in bed, asleep. A wafting mist hung between. The ghost of me felt no pain and no emotion. It was placid and unattached when it spoke the choices, "Allow yourself to die or succumb to the struggle of living with the pain. Find peace in the pain and become a child of peace within an imperfect world."

I wanted to be part of the world. I wanted to enjoy life and not feel the need to be someone. To just be, could I be that for a while, just awhile. There must be something else, something more, more joy and more laughter. The ghost of me floated back inside of my body. I accepted that the unknown was in front of me. That it would take days, months and possibly years to be emotionally and physically strong once again.

Rose awoke. The afternoon had turned to dusk. With her eyes still closed Rose felt the sickness, fatigue, sorrow and loss, but when she opened them to the house plants she had nurtured for years and the untouched forest only a step away from her home she felt the strength to continue.

For six months, in the darkness of night, Rose scribbled down the nightmares and dreams that haunted her. They let loose. She stopped waking up afraid, feeling that she was nowhere she wanted to be when she accepted the abyss as something that she had chose to fall into. It was where she needed to be. Life ached back. What she was changing into, Rose had no idea.

When the fear of death itself and the fear that she may choose to end her life took hold, Rose called the Silent Unity prayer line.

They were available 24/7. She could call as many times as she needed. It was OK. It took some time for her to truly believe it was acceptable. That it was a gift. There was a voice, someone always answered her call. Those prayers, so many prayers calmed her tenuous life. Every time they said God a gradual vibration penetrated the very center of her solar plexus.

> *The light of God surrounds you;*
> *The love of God enfolds you;*
> *The power of God protects you;*
> *The presence of God watches you;*
> *Where ever you are God is.*
>
> *James Dillet Freeman.*

Rose laid her hands on her belly and whispered to herself, "Don't give up," words that Russell said when the problems of her life seemed unbearable.

Two years, twice a week, housekeepers came and went with needs of their own. No one could compare to Alice. One arrived exactly on time, walked in without knocking, looked past Rose, said hello only because she had to, did the chores and then matter-of-factly said goodbye, her face closed and left. No more, no less. Another attempted to dominate Rose's environment with her philosophies of birth, life and death and without saying a word moved the furniture to her liking.

It took some time before Rose had the emotional and physical strength to speak to the housekeepers on her own behalf and make an attempt to be on her own once again.

After a year's worth of helpers stepping into her life, Rose reconnected to her ability to speak her truth diplomatically and straight to the point. "Don't move that. I like it there," to the housekeeper about to maneuver Rose's bookcase to the opposite corner of the room.

The housekeeper made an about-face and glared at Rose. In lightening speed she powered out, "Well! I get bored with furniture in the same place for more than a month. I move mine all the time."

Lying weak and needy in her bed Rose ordered, "I don't, leave it. This is my house."

The housekeeper let go of the bookcase. She shrugged her shoulders then went to the kitchen to yell, "It's your house."

From the bowels of her bed Rose declared, "That's right and I'm paying you."

With each statement of her truth, big or small, Rose's self-regard and body strengthened.

One day that month the said housekeeper left without a word. Rose called the agency when she didn't arrive the following scheduled day. Unbeknownst to Rose it had been the housekeeper's final day with her. She could tell that the woman had made up excuses. Rose chose not to ask questions, request another or make a complaint. To her, it wasn't worth it.

The longest to stay and kindest helper of them all was recommended by a friend. A retired ER nurse and longtime independent caregiver, Edward did what the former housekeepers did and more. He drove Rose to Ms. Mary Beam's home, a well-known and highly respected counselor in the area. Edward believed that she could assist Rose in sorting out her troubled mind.

Ms. Beam liked to be called Mary. She was the one and only counselor who addressed, with great integrity, the fact that Rose was oppressed by the shame of her childhood. The balance between emotional and physical health was discussed for weeks.

As a child, Rose held a deep sympathy for humanity. Her parents used it to turn her into their servant. A realization she had shoved into the recesses of her mind in order to survive.

Mary and Rose brought back Rose's self-regard in the most profound way. They delved into the seed of her low self-esteem. Her lack of an ability to honor her needs first was repeated over and over again in her life.

Every move she made was up to her. Don't engage in the power of those full of an agenda to control the talents she was blessed with. Sensitivity is a blessing not a curse. The power to discern good from evil was within her.

During one unforgettable session, Mary pulled out from behind her couch a large plastic bat. She set it next to Rose, placed half a dozen throw pillows on the floor and then suggested, "Pretend the pillows are your Mother and Father. What would you like to say or do to them? Use or don't use the bat. Speak to them honestly and directly. This is a sound proof room."

Instantly, Rose's forgotten strength uprooted itself. She grabbed the bat and beat the pillows with rage and fury over and over again. Dripping in sweat, her hot nerve pain spread throughout her sickened, oppressed, weak body. She screamed at the top of her lungs. "Why didn't you protect me? Why did I have to be your fucking maid? Why did you let that horrible man rape me? I hate, I hate you, I hate you!" over and over again until she had said it all.

Two flattened, blood and organ seeping bodies flashed before Rose's eyes. They were her parents. Dead. She had killed them. It terrorized her to know how good that felt. She was empowered and horrified by what she had done. The bat slipped onto the rug. Sobbing, "What have I done?"

Rose looked up to see Mary's smile. She wrapped her arms around Rose for a very long time and then ever so softly said, "Don't worry. You'll be OK. You released an anger that you held inside yourself for decades. You're not alone. I too have felt that kind of rage."

It was Rose's last session.

When Edward's car swung into Ms. Mary Beam's driveway, Rose had more positive energy coming out of her than she had in years.

Always considerate, he said, "How was it?" as Rose took her seat.

"Great! Thanks for asking."

Rose truly appreciated Edward, a lovely man inside and out. He was open to discussions of the emergency services pit falls that Mary and Rose had addressed at many a session. But the time had come for him to go. He, with his gift of gab, continued conversations long after they had discussed a topic to its end. Although Rose knew she would miss those last six months with him and had benefited from his assistance for the most basic of needs, she let him go in order to honor her healing process. She was done being taken care of.

Part Seven

One step at a time, I opened up to my strengths and how
they grew back when I did for myself. I was going to
get my life back no matter how long it took.

Rose went inward. It was where the answers to her questions lived.

Ufda, passed. She was thirteen years old, had been Rose's sidekick for all those years. She ached for her.

Now she's at the pond with her furry friends. She is fifty-two years old. Her horse, Lana, is twenty-four and her cat, Patches, is six. They're all gray and white either from age or they came into the world that way. Patches and Lana get that honor. Rose grew into her color. She is getting stronger after four years of willing herself well. Money is low.

The pond with all its surrounding grass just across the way from her home looked mighty appealing to all of them. Rose brought along her watch. Five in the evening was their time to go across the way to the inviting bowl of water. Lana shouldn't eat the rich thick grasses for more than an hour. It put her in danger of a tummy ache. Rose wouldn't let that happen.

Lana went straight into the pond all the way up to her knees. Her hooves grew long in the toe over the winter months. Rose hoped for a soft and easy way to get a free trim. A week of feedings at the pond softened Lana's hooves up just fine. She then walked the dry ground to trim them up. A farrier couldn't have done it better.

As the days of Lana's meals at the pond went by, Rose began to trust and let go of the thoughts of her horse getting into trouble. With great pleasure, she watched the wildlife that sought out a drink or a home at the pond. Frogs, ducks, wild turkeys, rabbits and countless dragonflies all gave her company and many lessons in the pleasures and survival techniques of this existence here on earth.

Rose had a bird feeder just outside her south facing windows. She had shaken the seeds to the ground for the doves and robins. Turkeys are land feeders and smart. A lone turkey came into Rose's life right as she turned the corner from the front door on her way to fetch Lana. The last of the prehistoric birds was eating under the feeder. To her delight, the turkey didn't rush away, but ever so slowly stepped through the bushes and then went overland in the direction of the pond. Rose rang out sweet and low, "Little turkey, hi little turkey."

She fetched Lana. Excited when it came to any prospect of thick juicy green grass on her horizon, Lana hurried Rose with whinnies and intermittent pulls on the rope.

Upon their arrival, Rose flung the rope over Lana's back. To then watch with a great appreciation her beautiful horse basking in the sun light and cooling her heels.

Rose sat herself down among the grass and relaxed with a book, pencil and paper and her cross-stitch project. In the distance, she caught a sweet glimpse of the turkey eating the tips of the grass bursting with seed filled pods. The bird was so much alone, but she seemed healthy, content. Rose identified with the little bird's solitary existence, enough to then lay back and allow her feelings to wash over her.

A blue heron, coyotes, the dozens and dozens of dragonflies and frogs were her companions that summer.

I was more at peace during those hours at the pond then I had ever known. I listened to my thoughts, where they took me and decided one thought at a time which ones could stay and which ones must go.

Five years after Rose left the Briggs Volunteer Fire Department, Chuck and Ethel were dead. The mind chatter had subsided, but images of the elderly couple's disabilities held on.

It was one of those hot and crisp and very dry August afternoons that Rose chose to take shaky measured steps the half mile down the road to the old beat up trailer. The weight of their slow demise on her shoulders, Rose dressed in her favorite summer's outfit: a straw hat, floral spaghetti strapped top, jean shorts and sandals.

Approaching the trailer, flashbacks came rolling in; the fore-boding pleas, the dingy cramped dwelling. Rose could still smell the must and body odor.

To get her bearings, she sat down on the splintered and buck-led wood porch. For a time she embraced herself with compassion and reassurance, then she willed herself upright and made the necessary effort to open the door. The rickety, paper-thin alumi-num door stopped her in her tracks. It was locked. She was kept from gazing upon the dismal world that Chuck and Ethel lived in at the end of their married life. A warm wind wafted over her, sooth-ing the haunting desperate needs of the couple. Rose's response, "I'll be right there," dissipated from her overcrowded mind.

I strolled home, a little lighter that day.

For months that turned into years, I started my car, let it run,
turned the Ignition off and then walked away.

Sammy held debilitating memories that Rose couldn't shake. To drive that car was a panic attack in the making. After numerous phone calls, her neighbor Beth offered to take her to town twenty miles away once a week for the supplies that the little grocery just didn't have.

Rose slowly emptied her savings account. With Cindy, her long time encouraging friend she applied for food stamps and MEDI-CAL. After mounds of paperwork she had proven that she was weak enough and worthy enough of the privilege of receiving Social Supplemental Income.

In the far corner of the grocery her loving friend and massage therapist Barbara, handed her a book, "Eat Right 4 Your Blood Type" by Peter J. D'Adamo with Catherine Whitney. "It may help," with a hug.

Having already read "Sugar Blues" and eliminating sugar from her diet, ready and willing to read whatever nutritional books she could get her hands on. Rose accepted it with gratitude. It was her dietary bible. Every meal, every grocery list was determined by that book.

She put herself on a cleaning schedule, one room a day in an energy available rotation with her town trip.

In her twenties as a student of ballet and modern dance, Rose learned the long laborious process of physical fitness. Now she walked everyday. At little at first, then bit by bit she extending her walk further and further each week to her goal, two miles. She choreographed a personalized exercise routine to bring back an old familiar limberness and find her center.

After six months, Beth stopped being available for town trips. The social pressure in their small community had mounted to a point that she couldn't withstand. Few believed Rose could recover.

Rose was a recluse, looking about, seeing much, revealing little.

The hardest of all performances, to be strong enough to withstand the negative forces of the world knowing that there were those who drove her road, who thought that she was dying or hoped she was dead.

With the determination of a tiger recovering from a severe injury Rose hauled herself down her short dirt road. The moment she turned onto the main road the self-effacing task of possibly hitch-hiking in full view of Heath Mat struck her head on. Her heart pounded deep in her chest and her breath was shallow, but she lifted her arm and put up her thumb. When an undesirable vehicle closed in, her intuition welled up from the depths of her self-worth. She put her arm down, made no eye contact and let them go by. Kind souls stopped, welcomed her in and asked how she was doing. Words of support or knowing silence carried her to her most basic of needs.

The feeling of being adrift in a crowd of acquaintances from a life left behind grabbed her guts. Simple talk filled her with fear. It was all she could do to gather up the food, put it in the basket, wait for the groceries to be bagged up, hand the cashier her food stamps or cash framed in shame and then come up with the simplest of words, "Thank You." With nothing more to say she slipped out of the newly foreign yet so familiar grocery store. She had no choice but to acknowledge the fact that she was a person she hardly recognized.

Rose put up her thumb.

Her father's evil ways haunted her still, but he had ingrained practical common sense in Rose. Once home, she divided the food into seven equal days of meals. A lesson learned long ago from him. She put them away, prepared a snack then sat down knowing that if she didn't eat she would die. It served her well, but it was not he who made her choices now.

It was me.

Rose got back in her car and sat until the shakes subsided. She told herself, "You're only going a few miles to the gas station and grocery. The beeper didn't go off. You don't have one anymore. No emergencies. You're not a public servant." Looking into the back seat, no medical emergency bag sat ready and waiting to save anyone's life. She allowed herself to be absolutely indifferent to the fate of others.

Rose wasn't ready to trust herself completely. Nonetheless, she made herself drive her, struggling to run, car to her appointments if and only if they were less than five miles away. Her desire to be independent drove her to drive the two miles to the bus stop. Breathing exercises helped keep her calm in the close and tight environment of the bus. She made some friends and went to a chiropractor, and an applied kinesiologist, an allergist and a massage therapist whose offices were at least twenty miles from her home. She was worth it.

For years to come, Rose took the bus, not excepting assistance from many of her small town community members. She sensed in them a gossip-driven drive to help.

Three years of hard work stabilized my health.

Its ongoing assurance appeared in the form of a cat. Although Rose had lost Patches to a territory hungry neighboring cat, her need to care for one continued. Her next cat must live inside. Losing a cat to wildlife or the cats that lived steps away was unacceptable.

Her friend Cindy was called the cat lady. She tended to any stray cat that crossed her path. Bless her heart, she caught them and then took them to the vet to be spayed in bulk. The ones that she could coerce into her home became hers.

Cindy had taken Rose to the doctor a number of times when she was far too weak to drive. She still visited from time to time. On such a visit she had a long haired feline, white with bits of gray, in a cage in her car. Rose had to say hi, ask about the cat and what her plans were with this one.

"She's yours if you want. Not sure if she's fixed. She looks healthy. About a year I'd say. Want her?"

"Maybe, yes, I'm ready."

"You are."

The cat was fixed. Rose paid her friend for her trouble. Cindy was ecstatic.

Their next meeting Cindy said shaking her head with a smirk, "You're easy."

Rose declared, "Not really. I was ready."

The cat's name came about when Rose was meandering about her home. "Lily" floated into her mind like a soft blanket of lily pads.

Rose and Lily got used to one another and each other's ways. A so very small lithe being in her home stabilized the inner workings of Rose's life.

I was estranged from my family, but the tap root wouldn't die.

Rose needed money. She knew some loggers from her days in the fire service. One in particular bought pine trees. Their familiar faces and willingness to give her advice made the project possible.

Getting out from under the gloom that hung over Rose's home was a priority. Her house was lightless for the ever growing pine and oak trees that shaded her home. All so grand when the blazing heat of summer was kept at bay by all the limbs, needles and leaves. But when winter set in the shade brought with it a prolonged darkness and a fear of falling trees. The threat hammered on Rose's tenuous peace of mind.

Arrangements were made. The logger would arrive to give her an estimate and set a time to do the work. Rose Okayed it. She was going to sell some trees, a lot of trees. She had over twenty that caught the logger's eye.

SSI and side jobs had kept her going for four years. She always claimed those side jobs. It was a matter of pride with her. Selling those trees would give her a bundle. The neighbors weren't too keen on it, but it was her land to do with as she wished. She needed the money, sun in the winter and her stout oaks to thrive.

It was February. The heaviest weather covered Rose's world. The trees were to be removed the following spring. She could handle the gloom one more season.

As of late, lots of calls had come and gone from Rose's home. When it rang that late February morning she thought nothing of who it might be. A voice so familiar yet so little heard. It was Stanley. Rose's gut went tight. It was business. Money owed her from their mother's estate. He was the executor. Mother had insisted. She didn't trust Art. Rose understood.

She was extremely grateful to get the money, very grateful in fact, but Stanley didn't sound right. Her long left behind experience as an Emergency Medical Service person pushed to the forefront of her mind. It was imperative that she find out what his health status was. She began a long list of loaded questions.

"It's hard to breathe? Are you having chest pain? What kind of food do you crave? How do you feel after a night's sleep? How well do you sleep?"

Things didn't look good for Stanley.

In a slow even tone Rose said, "I appreciate you taking the time to call and make this right with Mother's estate. But from what you've just told me. You need to call 911. It's much more important."

Rose wanted to do for her younger brother, but she feared his angry response to her would rise up. She'd be left with the sounds of him having a heart attack.

Stanley never failed to remember how much I loved my collection of 45s. I collected every Ricky Nelson record available and then some.

To my surprise, during one of my few and far between visits he took my partner Dean and me to Los Angeles for a Ricky Nelson concert.

Twenty-one years after I moved away, he sent me my 45s safe and in excellent condition.

When our mother died Stanley's lack of personal care accelerated.

He loved ear blasting music. With money he earned he bought record albums, adding to his huge collection, went to rock concerts and slam-danced. Our phone conversations were all about the greatest band of the time. I just listened, happy that he had a passion, a quest, a joy to fulfill his life. Although I rarely knew what band he was talking about I never let on. I thought, "Why spoil the moment?"

Rose was Stanley's last family connection that showed any kind of honesty, respect and acceptance. They had many conversations the last four months of his life. They spoke of their time together as kids, her logging project, public transportation issues, health, cleanliness and its value. Rose hoped beyond the odds that he would get better, if only he would listen.

Not until after an extended period of time in a rest home with Stanley hearing the same words from the nurses did he say to Rose, "I didn't understand what you meant about healthy eating and personal hygiene, now I do."

Rose was glad, but it was too late.

During their very short conversation only hours before his death, Rose told him how much she loved him and how sorry she was to have left him alone with Mother and Father.

He said, "Yeah," real gentle.

That one word alone said with that tone in his voice opened a door to the past. The world that Stanley and Rose lived in when who they were to become hadn't come to be was there before her. It was the word he said over and over to her when they were kids and she was trying, so hard, to find out what he really thought and felt about his life and the world around him.

Stanley died in the hospital. He was fifty-three years old, diagnosed with malnourishment, diabetes and congestive heart failure. There was nothing Rose could have done. All were malfunctions of the body that took years to acquire. Rose had to accept that the lifestyle he had succumbed to did what it did to him. But it broke her heart.

On his death bed Stanley was surrounded by his paperwork and portable radio. The stock market was at an all time high that day. Money was his power. He left the earth at the peak of what he valued most.

He was eccentric, hardworking, obsessive, responsible, diplomatic, money savvy to the point of fearful greed, socially inadequate, a devoted public transportation passenger, collector of train, bus schedules and coupons and unbelievably condescending when others didn't share his knowledge.

Rose's sensitive digestive tract was the weak link in her health. When Stanley was dying she struggled to maintain any as semblance of normalcy.

After lengthy conversations with Stanley followed by unwanted, controlling phone calls from her estranged older brother Art, over Stanley's estate, her nerves had had it. They were the kind of phone calls that strip away one's elusive belief that the world is a safe place to live.

It was ten years since Rose's nervous breakdown. A sense of dread of what this situation could do to her was in the forefront of her mind. All the words of wisdom from her extended family and a chiropractor-medical intuitive that she'd been seeing for years came into play. She prayed and then let go of the decisions daily, but Rose wouldn't allow Art and his family to override the law. And they tried.

They all lived in southern California, miles and miles away from her rural world. She was experienced in the area of health care, but she was too far away to assist with the care of her younger brother. She had accepted that. Moreover, the residue of her frantic life as a firefighter/EMT stopped her. It was not to her benefit to get too involved regardless of her experience. Rose held back her opinions or simply gave advice only when asked, reminding herself that it wasn't up to her, Art and Stanley had karma to work out that had nothing to do with her.

Late one, thick with heat, night Art relayed the news. The long wait for Stanley's home (the old family house) to be sold was over.

Art and his family wanted more money than it was worth. Following a battle of wills Rose received the money she was due. She got what she believed was right, the right to live the simple life that she craved.

She had left that house, full of childhood memories, over forty years ago. It was no longer in her world. There was no place that she had any connection to from that time. Rose could let go.

Self-help was her beacon in the sea of troubles clouding her life, but her intestines suffered. Her diet had long been a top priority. It stabilized her, but the emotional upheavals kept her in knots.

Early the next morning, as she lay in bed in the yoga corpse pose, the contents of her intestines moved like the ocean, ebbing and flowing from one pipe to another.

"Why?" Rose wondered. She'd been eating the same all along.

To find the answer Rose removed herself emotionally from what was happening to her body. The logic was clear. She was about to purge the memories, tightness and seemingly endless fear of her own existence.

She thought, "I live alone. I have my life to live, an extended family and animals that depend on me for their survival. My prayers were answered. The house is sold. All the phone conversations were worth it. Let it go."

Her innards were about to empty. She rushed down the stairs to the bathroom. She made it. Black green diarrhea spurt out of her. Glued to the toilet seat, terrified and trembling, she relived the last months. When she was finally empty, she mustered up the energy to shuffle her way to the sofa, lie down and wait out the terror.

After a few hours, Rose called a health care provider who knew her case well. He confirmed her diagnosis. With kindness and care in his voice he said, "You experienced an emotional release. The liver is the seat of anger. The color of your diarrhea was your liver cleansing itself. You're fine. Just rest."

Rose did, with peace in her heart.

Months later, at Stanley's estate sale Rose was informed by his neighbors how much he loved to share his thoughts and feelings with his friends.

Rose was happy that he had found them. She regrets not spending more time with him. She had to forget him. Most important, they didn't have much of a chance. He lived where she couldn't be.

One chilly clear day, Rose was outside her home raking leaves in the soothing air that accompanied the autumn of Stanley's death. For no particular reason she lifted her gaze to see his essence floating up to her, "You've got a great place here. Sorry I didn't take the time to visit. I am glad you got some money. Knowing you, you'll be able to live on it for the rest of your life in a simple down-to-earth way."

In a whisper, Rose said to Stanley, "Thanks for stopping by," continuing to rake the leaves all the while remembering raking the loose grass to the sidewalk when my younger brother and I did yard work together as kids.

There is always injustice and possible loss, do what you can to change the situation. No matter what is right or true you cannot change what people do.

Except it and go your way.
Eileen Connolly

It was time for me to extend the boundaries of my life.
I went to a friend.

It was the year Stanley's estate was settled. Rose was driving more, but never far. Panic attacks still crept in at the most unexpected times. Little vacations that she once took to the neighboring small town of Cottonwood with her dog Ufda, to escape work, Dean and the fire service drifted back into her mind. Her friend Seth worked there. Maybe she could hitch a ride with him for the day.

The oak leaves that surround Rose's home turned to a straw yellow. Sun made its' appearance later each day. Cooling temperatures and erratic winds spoke of the coming of winter.

Rose's dear friend Seth was to meet with her at the Pine Creek Elementary School. Their public service years, although in different facets, where full of promise and idealism. This empathic man washed over her with sunshine. He had crawled into her head in the kindest of ways for over twenty years. Chatter within her mind made it a challenge to relax. She didn't want to embarrass her charitable and reserved friend in the slightest. To an even greater degree, she needed to be comfortable in her own skin. After much deliberation, she picked out a cap-sleeved silk blouse, the floral print in deep red, cream and sage. A sleeveless cotton sweater of burgundy with ruffles at the hips, her favorite blue jeans and sandals finished the ensemble. She felt good.

Seth sped into the parking lot in his sporty car, the car of her dreams, a forest-green Mazda Miata and came to an abrupt halt. With his unmistakable charm and warm tone he said, "I saw you speeding down the road in your VW, then you disappeared, glad I found you. I was parked on the lower road doing some paperwork, last minute changes. You get that Bug of yours moving pretty fast."

Rose was frightened at the very idea of going out beyond her mental boundaries to simply enjoy the afternoon. She was frozen in place, her backside sealed, glued against the outside of her car. She was about to make up some excuse to forgo the day, but she willed herself to circle around his vehicle, crank open the door and slide down onto the seat. She allowed herself to be absorbed within the womb of his car then she responded, "Yes I do... Were you waiting for a long time? Sorry I'm late."

Reassuring Seth responded, "You're not. Are you ready?"

Rose relaxed, "Yes. Let's go. It's a beautiful drive."

With regret Seth said, "I rarely get a chance to enjoy it. Most of the time, I'm preoccupied with family, work, the usual, but you're right. It's a beautiful drive."

They were zipping down the road when Seth politely asked, "Am I driving too fast?" with a trace of worry.

Rose was, to her relief, at ease, "No."

But then they approached an unmistakable curve in the road. A flash, a memory, a horrific accident flew into Rose's mind. Two teenagers died. The driver survived. Chief Heath Mat had tugged and yanked her, the EMT-defibulator-in-hand, back and forth from one boy with no pulse to another. Rose shivered that warm morning as they slipped past the now empty space where only memories lived.

Seth let out, "Rose, are you OK? You just shivered," taking his foot off the accelerator.

After taking in a few long deep breathes she responded, "Thanks for asking. We just passed the scene of an auto-accident that has haunted me for years."

Seth put on the gas and then declared, "I remember. I drove by. I thought of stopping, but you were sitting and talking with a guy from the department on the tail gate of a truck. You looked really sad. Sorry we had to go this way."

Rose accepted her responsibilities, "It's OK. I need to let it go. I'll come here on my own. It'll help."

Seth said, "Do," in a way that warmed Rose's heart.

Set adrift from the flashback and struggling to hold on to her dream of a lovely day Rose couldn't think clearly enough to say another word. She wanted, needed from the depth of her gut to forget the pain that wouldn't let go. For twenty miles they sat close wrapped up in their own thoughts.

Breaking the silence, Seth questioned, "Have you eaten or should I say, would you like to have lunch with me? My cases don't go before the judge for a couple of hours."

"Yes, I'd like that very much." A jolt of happiness pierced Rose, giving her the courage to say, "May I watch you be a lawyer?"

To the point, Seth responded, "Sure, but there are some cases that are private, you'll be required to sit out in the lobby."

Privacy, a world Rose knew a great deal about gave her voice to her words, "I understand. That's not a problem."

In one of the booths of the local restaurant, Sadie's Bar and Grill. Seth and Rose sat face to face. He opened his briefcase and pulled out paperwork.

Seth moved his gaze to Rose saying, "I wish I wasn't so preoccupied."

Taking in the atmosphere and settled in her seat, Rose said, "It's OK. You're in work-mode."

Comforted within the understanding of Seth's need to ready himself for his day in court, Rose ordered her meal.

After their food was delivered they sat in mutual silence, lost in the world behind their eyes for some time. Then a few of Seth's colleagues strolled in and gathered around the far table. He pointed them out, explaining who they were in relationship to the court system.

Seth rose, "Be right back," strolled over to one of his female colleagues and said, "It's good to see you. I heard you left, but I wasn't told why."

She smiled a warm smile, briefly touched his shoulder then responded, "It's good to see you too. I had personal business to attend to. It's been taking up a lot of my time."

Seth titled his head, took a step in her direction then put into words his heartfelt appreciation, "Thank you for your support when things got rough. I've missed you. Good luck," followed by a farewell hug.

Rose thought, "She means a lot to him," comforted in the knowing that Seth had supportive friends in his life.

He hadn't finished his food, but needed to go.

Rose offered, "Can I leave your sandwich off at your apartment or bring it with me to the courthouse?"

In a hurry, Seth said, "My apartment," explained how to get there, left some money on the table and rushed out the door saying, "Come by the courthouse at 2pm. There's only one chamber. You'll find me."

In no time the waitress came back, "Sorry I didn't introduce myself, I'm Laura. Can I get you anything else?"

Rose was in Seth's world. He was known and when she was in an unfamiliar circumstance she always error to the side of caution. "Hi, I'm Rose. Seth and I are old friends. I've been acquainted with him and his wife and daughter for years. Would you please put his sandwich in a to-go-bag?"

Laura said with an air of respect and fondness for her friend, "He's a good man. He had it rough the last couple of years. There are some members of this community that wanted his job."

Rose stated, "Seth is allowing me to stay in his apartment next week while he's out of town with his family. For many a summer, I came here with my dog for a much needed vacation. I haven't been able to for years." She took a sip of water, fumbled with the money Seth had left behind. "I never read any of the newspaper articles that address the problems you're referring to. I only know what Seth has chosen to share with me. Yes, he's a good man, one of the best."

"I'll bag up Seth's sandwich for you, be right back." In what felt like seconds Laura was back, bag in hand, "It was nice to meet you. I hope I get a chance to see you next week. I work Thursday, Friday and Saturday," leaving the luncheon bill in a paper cup.

Rose put money in the cup, collected her things and Seth's to-go-bag and then left to find the apartment.

When Rose pulled open the side door of one of the local businesses a long, steep stairway greeted her anxious spirit. She made her way in the dark to the top. In a flash, the lights that were connected to the sensor ignited. There were three doors to choose from. Her memory was fuzzy, but she recalled it was "never locked."

The first door to the right was unlocked. Rose tentatively opened the door. The apartment was filled to the brim with antiques, not unlike Seth's home in Briggs, but there was an out-spoken rainbow parrot perched in the corner on top of its cage.

Momentarily paralyzed and a bit queasy Rose thought, "Is this his apartment? It could be, but the bird. He's never said a word about a bird."

Nonetheless she visited with the squawking bird, left the to-go-bag on the kitchenette table then went for a stroll.

The little town was bustling with midday activities. People Rose didn't recognize walked here and there. It was a pleasure to be a tourist, free and open to observe.

At 2pm, enclosed within an aura of politeness, on guard and acutely aware of her surroundings, Rose approached the looming courthouse and then stepped inside. The interior of the building was furnished with heirlooms from the early 1900's. A plaque on the wall announcing the chamber led the way. She climbed the stairway that led to the small lobby just outside the chamber of the county seat.

Men and women sat on hard wooden benches with their heads hanging down, starring at nothing on the floor. A couple of them put their hand on the knee of or wrapped an arm around the one sitting next to them. Others sat alone. Silent anger, fear, hope and countless questions filled the room. Rose momentarily settled among them and tried to unearth what was about to happen, but after a deep self-reassuring breath she got up and opened the chamber's door. The law enforcement officer standing just inside the doorway allowed her to come in. Rose sat in the back. No sign of Seth.

From the side door, directly connected to the front of the room, Seth, protected by the bailiff, entered the room with ease.

The judge faced Rose and all those who were participating in the trial of the accused. Agitated, but steady and comforted within her own silence Rose watched.

She reassured herself, "I'm a part of this world for a very short time. Don't bring unnecessary attention to yourself."

In his full presence as a lawyer, Seth took a seat facing and left of the judge. A heavy-set man in his forties clothed in a dark orange jumper with INMATE stamped on the back was brought out, in handcuffs, and sat down next to Seth Preston, Public Defender-Stratton County. Seth leaned toward his client, whispered reassuring words then put his hand on the inmate's upper back. Rose was touched.

Her friend, the public defender, in a role she'd never witnessed before, stood straight and tall in his pinstriped suit then declared, "He is not a danger to himself or others. We are in a safe environment. He is not going to flee. There is no need for him to be restrained at this time."

The judge gave the bailiff a nod. The inmate stood up allowing access to the handcuffs. He sat quietly.

Seth eloquently informed the judge, "William Ames will continue to follow all requirements requested of him including monthly visits to his probationary officer."

The judge agreed and allowed the inmate to leave under his own recognizance, but only after he made the necessary arrangements.

Rose admired Seth's way with the judge, bailiff and his client. She had witnessed the simple truth. Her friend was fulfilling his calling, to help the wayward unfortunate people of our society with kindness, intelligence and the empathic perspective of a humanitarian.

Believing in the fate of others as well as her own she realized, "Somehow he must find and use the logic within the framework of the law to keep him going and not give up."

More cases followed.

Eventually, the bailiff turned to face the onlookers then announced, "A case of a personal nature is about to commence.

All those uninterested in the following case please leave the courtroom."

Rose stood. Her mind shifted to a time when she too sat outside a courtroom.

I was a frightened to death, plump, pimple faced, fourteen year old girl waiting to see if I was needed to testify against the man who had raped me for a total of three years.

He pleaded guilty to a lesser charge. I didn't testify. He got-off with a fine and two years probation. It left me stunned, betrayed, angry and tainted.

It happened over forty years ago. Back then rape was swept under the rug and assumed that the victim was at fault.

Rose needed to and did experience a different and most important positive perspective of the courtroom. That one afternoon with her friend the lawyer changed her life.

After all of Seth's cases were over for the day Rose went back to the lobby. She overheard a young man complaining about his lawyer. "He's no good. He said he'd get me off, but he didn't."

The very next minute, Seth appeared. A brief look of recognition passed between Rose and Seth then he fixed his eyes directly into those of the young man and said, "Are you fulfilling the judge's requests? Moreover, why are you here? I'm done for the day. Next time, if there is a next time, I can't help you. Remember that!"

Seth and Rose started to leave, but then a medium built guy in his early thirties dressed in threadbare work clothes and smelling of oil and sweat wedged his way through the crowd of people on their way down the stairs. He tapped Seth on the shoulder then spoke as friends do direct and familiar, "Seth has my friend's case gone before the judge?"

Stiffness formed around his mouth. He shot daggers into the guy's eyes. "Seth Preston, attorney at law."

"Sorry! I know William Ames. Does he need a ride?"

Even toned, Seth said, "You need to talk to the bailiff, or better yet, go to the jail. Your friend is most likely filling out or recently completed his paperwork for his release."

Rose thought, "Don't say a word. This is none of your business," acknowledging Seth's position.

Outside the courtroom their energy softened. Rose walked proud next to her friend's graceful stride. He explained his world a little more.

Seth had a rug in his car to unload and take up to his apartment. To assist, Rose opened the side door of the building. She followed him to the top of the stairs. Now shoulder to shoulder she opened the first door to the right.

Seth exclaimed, "What are you doing? Close that door. I specifically told you my apartment is at the end of the hallway!"

Rose flushed, hung her head then trailed him down the hallway to his door. It opened up to a sun drenched spacious apartment furnished in family heirlooms and memorabilia. Large healthy geraniums and Christmas cactus added breathe to Seth's world away from home.

He dropped the rug on the floor and showed her around, all the while explaining the workings of the apartment.

"Would you water my plants?

"Sure, I'd be happy to."

"Hey, I'm hungry. Where's my sandwich?"

Rose wasn't all together sure what to do, but she was with the most empathic person she knew. Embarrassed she explained, "There may be a problem. I left your sandwich in the other apartment."

An ever ready problem solver Seth exclaimed with restraint, "Go get it. That's my landlord's place. If we're lucky he hasn't discovered it. He's a sweet understanding man, but..."

Walking down the dismal hallway Rose prayed he was right. She knocked on the landlord's door, no answer. She crept in, looked for the sandwich. It was gone! Distraught, she tiptoed down the hallway.

Rose shrank inside, "What am I going to do? I've really blown it."

In response to the news Seth took a couple of steps away from Rose, looked out the window, sighed and then turned to say, "We have to go downstairs and talk to my landlord. He's in his shop."

Rose whispered, "I'm so sorry."

She dreaded facing her judge and jury, but she had no choice.

Entering the shop a kind soft-spoken man acknowledged Seth with a free and easy manner, "Hi Seth, how's the world of law and order?"

"Moving right along. Good to see you. I'd like to introduce you to Rose. Rose is the woman I mentioned to you last month. She will be staying in my apartment next week. By the way, did you find a to-go-bag in your apartment?"

The landlord's face opened up to a larger than life smile that hardly fit on his face. "So that was YOUR sandwich, I thoroughly enjoyed it. I left the pickle. Do you want the pickle? Just kidding, I have it right here." He turned, looked under the counter then presented the sandwich.

Rose thought, "Shit, what am I suppose to say?"

Deliberate, kind and caring Seth said, "We are, or should I say Rose is very sorry to have mistaken your apartment for mine."

Lighthearted the landlord responded, "Impossible. Mine is stuffed full of furniture. How she imagined mine to be yours is beyond me. You'd think the bird alone would have been a red-flag."

Seth smirked, "Well she did," looking to the floor and shaking his head.

"Now we know where the delicious looking sandwich came from. My wife and I called every restaurant in this god-forsaken small town to find its owner. It's the talk of the town." He chuckled. "Not really! We were very careful not to mention your name. In fact, we didn't even think of you. People around here love to play pranks."

Rose said, "And now you know for sure that I've never been in Seth's apartment. I never would have made such a dreadful mistake if I had," wishing she'd kept her mouth shut.

"It's OK Seth, the apartment is yours to use as you choose, within reason of course. My wife and I can't imagine you making any problems for us."

The landlord's shining eyes drifted to her. "It was nice to meet you."

Rose let go of her fears. "It was nice to meet you."

Seth and Rose ambled back up to his apartment and completed the tour.

Then they loaded themselves back into his car and drove up the road that led directly to the back-roads.

Only a few miles out of town they stopped to take in a multi-tiered mystical waterfall. White water flowed over rounded smooth with time boulders, dropped elongated curtains of water that collected in pools then overflowed over and over again. They hiked to the falls, allowed the mist on their faces to clean the day's mishaps away.

Seth breathed his words, "I've forgotten how beautiful these places are. When I come to Cottonwood it's all about work."

They were ready to move on. They climbed back into the car and drove up the road to the end of the pavement and beyond. Pine, cedar and oak trees stood straight and tall on both sides of the road.

"This is an excellent place to walk or run for miles and see practically no one. It's one of my running routes. Being that it's not far from town I can get a good run in before court."

"I would do the same if I lived and worked here. Back in the day when I was a horsewoman this would have been a perfect place to ride... By the way, Laura and I talked a bit after you left. Nice lady."

"What did she say?"

"That you're a good man. You do your best and often more than expected. Some people don't appreciate you. They don't have any idea how hard you work. You never complain. I agreed. I told her you're one of the kindest people I know."

"Thank you."

"You're very welcome."

It appeared to Rose that most of who Seth is was wrapped up in the courtroom, on the phone with a client or at his desk doing paperwork for their cases. She was aware that Seth's occupation deeply stressed him, but the thought of suggesting to him to limit what he is doing to relieve some of the stress was filled with complications. Care as she did, she knew in the depths of her heart that is wasn't her place to say a word.

Seth and Rose drove to another one of his running routes, a remote, but paved one-lane curved road miles from his home, apartment and the courtroom. As they drove along the route he pointed out distance markers and expressed how frustrated he was when one day a marker didn't show up right at the moment he needed to and thought it was time to turn back.

"Rose, I thought I had missed it. I kept looking and looking, but the next marker I saw was the number after the one I was looking for. I thought I was losing it."

"That would be frustrating. I'd feel the same way."

They stopped at the top of the hill, got out of the car, took in the panorama of tall pine, oak and cedar that carpeted the hilltops down to the river canyon below. They were acutely aware of the only moving sound for miles and miles. It was a logging truck in the distance. Seth stood yards away from Rose. Rose longed to sit on the railing and talk and talk, but the question of what to say hung in the air like thick fog.

Nonetheless, Rose brought up her money worries. It was mostly the suggestions of others to sell her house that nagged at her.

A knowing permeated his response, "Don't do it. In time you'll regret it. There's no legal reason for you to do it. You don't have to. You worked so hard, too hard to pay it off. Hold on. What would happen to Lana? She needs you. You need her. Stay."

"I'll try."

"Please do. You have a lovely home."

On the final leg back to her car, Seth shared a childhood talent that was still intact. He could recite the complete "Superman" theme song from the TV series back when they were kids.

Thrilled at the very idea of it, Rose belted out, "Wow, that's amazing, how about right now?"

But before Seth let loose, Rose had to calm her ardent enthusiast response for the old TV shows, especially "Superman." She summoned her inner calm and then allowed him to muster the nerve, focus and willingness to share.

All of a sudden, without warning, sweet Seth sang out:

>"Up in the sky! Look!
>It's a bird!
>It's a plane!
>It's Superman!
>Yes, it's Superman--strange visitor from the planet Kryton who came to Earth with powers and abilities far beyond those of mortal men.
>Superman, who can leap tall buildings in a single bound, race a speeding bullet to its target, bend steel in his bare hands,
>and who, disguised as Clark Kent, mild-mannered reporter for a great Metropolitan newspaper, fights a never-ending battle
>for truth and justice."

Creators Jerry Siegel and Joe Shuster
Announcer-narrator Jackson Beck

"Seth that was great. Thanks."

He said, "You're welcome," with a grin.

The remainder of the journey was quiet.

Rose's car was in sight. She succumbs to the fact. An afternoon outside her bubble of hibernation was over.

They came to a halt. Rose faced Seth, "Thank you for your day," and then moved to give him a hug, but he, ever so slightly, moved away and presented his hand.

Rose sunk. Unable to thank him in the way she hoped hurt a little. She responded in kind, looked down and then gathered up her things, "It's time for me to go."

Seth's feelings were disguised behind his sunglasses when he said, "I'll call you with the details."

Rose slipped out the door. He sped off.

Rose drove her beloved car, Sammy, the twenty miles to Cottonwood. Her inner voice repeating, "You'll be fine. There's no emergency, keep moving," sweeping over her like a warm comforting breeze. For one week, Rose the tourist, thanks to her friend, had a grand time.

> *Your friend is your needs answered.*
> *Kihlil Gibran*

The greatest gift you can give the world is a healthy you.
Carolyn Myss

Rose was about to complete her fifty-eighth year. She missed having a dog. Her walking stride was strong and steady. The tail wagging, sniffing about and egging her on of a dog was ever present. She asked around, but... Inadequacy raised its ugly head. Was she capable of watching over a canine? Her home, horse, cat and most important herself was plenty.

On a clear cold and crisp February afternoon, a gray four legged figure crossed into Rose's land and then settled near her back door. A husky-wolf was scrounging for food. Thrown scraps of vegetables and fruit for the wildlife brought the stray dog to her world. It was emaciated. Slowly wobbling from one place to the next, the thick molted haired animal was covered with a thin layer of dirt. Its tail was hanging down between its legs. Try as she did to convince herself to shoo it away. It wasn't possible. She opened the door just a crack and peered out.

The dog jolted then froze. With dull and foggy eyes it looked directly at Rose, hung its head and trembled.

Rose had absolutely no idea where the dog came from. It had been years since she had cared for a sick human much less a dog. She thought long and hard, "Could I give this dog what it needed? How sick is it? Would it bring harm to my pets or me?"

Remembering all that she had done for others and how aware she was of the body's ability to heal. Animals had and continued to be an essential part of her life. They were her children. She was not going to ignore this dog.

Rose needed to win its trust if she was going to be of assistance. She foraged around the kitchen for any food that might interest the forlorn dog. Ever so slowly she opened the door and tiptoed down the back steps. The dog eyed her. Rose crouched down on one knee and then extended her treat filled, open palmed hand. Longing for any small morsel, the timid dog elongated its neck and sniffed the air. Rose saw that the dog had a thick heavy metal choke collar around its neck. In faith, she believed the dog wouldn't bite or even growl at her. She made her move. In one lightening fast gesture she snatched the collar with her other hand, latched her leash, long left in the closet, to the dog's collar and then tugged. Stiff of body, the dog followed in measured steps.

Rose offered it some food. To her dismay the starving dog sniffed it, but wouldn't eat a bit. It appeared to be used to scraps it found in places Rose will never know. She gave the dog a bowl of water, a handful of kibble, an old horse blanket to lie on and then left it alone on the porch tied to a railing.

Experienced as a dog owner, Rose believed the dog needed to settle in, relax and come to accept her as its temporary guardian. Throughout the day and into the night, she checked on the dog, made sure to replace any food or water it chose to eat and took it for little walks.

Rose made every effort to find its owner. She wrote out small notes, posted them around town and made calls to the right people.

After four days with no response and neighbors reminding her that people who abandon dogs usually don't care to find them, Rose reassigned herself to be the dogs devoted caregiver.

She began the tedious task of bringing the dog back to health. First, she provided it with a bed of horse blankets and food and fresh water three times a day. The yet to bark, whine or growl dog eventually showed a willingness to accept her offerings.

The first time Rose allowed the dog into her home it relieved itself right in front of her. Completely taken aback Rose accidently dropped a piece of pineapple. The dog rushed over, gobbled it up and begged for more. Rose was puzzled as to why it would even consider eating pineapple. She had already witnessed the lack of healthy food in its diet and seen how weak and shaky it was physically. By the look of it, the dog hadn't eaten well for days or even months. Its stools were full of intestinal parasites. It had a serious case of diarrhea and definitely needed a strong dose of de-wormer to completely rid it of the parasites that were pulling the life force out of its body. But Rose felt that the dog's intestinal system was far too weak to handle the strength of a prescribed medication. So, to be extra safe, Rose gave it the de-wormer that the grocery store had to offer even though it was not as effective.

A distant, unaffectionate and insecure dog, it was time for Rose to become a strong alpha figure in the dog's life. After it allowed her to come near enough to pet and groom, she removed countless ticks all through its head, neck, chest and pits. Grease and dirt covered the sad dog's coat. As much as the dog allowed, Rose brushed it, but it was far too timid and frightened to bathe.

In only a couple of days it relaxed to her touch and lay down on its side. The orphaned dog was a girl. She needed a name. In one of Rose's dreams she lived alone in a rustic cabin on the prairies of Nebraska with her little girl named Annie. Rose knew that if she had ever had a baby girl she would have given the baby her very favorite name, Annie. The needy dog deserved the love she felt for her little girl in the prairies' of her dreams.

Rose needed a purpose. She left behind her driven idealistic self to heal. Skills lying dormant were ignited. Her self-esteem heighted, just a little more, by the simple acts of welcoming Annie into her life.

They started taking short walks. Rose taught Annie the most important commands: come, sit, stay, down and heel. She was slow to respond to every command except "down". Annie was already leash trained. She didn't pull Rose as they walked. She stayed near. With no command from Rose, Annie lay down when Rose stopped to talk to her neighbors and friends. It was comforting. Someone took the time to teach her something. A trip to the veterinarian was in order, but Rose didn't know if Annie knew how to ride in a car. Step-by-step she taught her how to load in and out of as well as be a passenger in her Bug. At the beginning, Rose got into the back seat first and then firmly pulled on the leach. All the while saying, "Come," over and over again in a commanding and kind voice. Although Annie resisted with a strength that Rose questioned she could match. Patience won over.

To her delight, Annie lay quiet. Rose started up the car and drove a few miles and then parked. To then go for a short walk and loaded up for the ride home. After a week of repeating the process every day Rose felt comfortable enough to take Annie to the vet.

With only a little nudge Annie allowed the vet to give her lots of shots. The greatest gift of all was a "well done" to Rose from the vet. "Come back in a couple of weeks."

After ten days, Annie's strength was back. Rose was so pleased with herself that she invited her friend Beth, to lunch to meet her new found dog friend.

It seemed that Annie was attached to Rose and her home. So the next day Rose left the dog untied when she went to the corner store for supplies.

Upon her return, there was no dog to greet her. Disbelief followed by a profound sadness soaked into her being.

A few hours later, Rose received a call from Beth. Without mincing one single word she yelled, "Your dog is walking down my road. Come get it!"

Annie hadn't identified with her name. Her response to "come" was sluggish or non-existent. Rose knew the possibility of catching her was slim to none. Rose's stomach tightened for the loss of what she hoped would be. She attempted detachment and then said, "The dog may be going home for all I know. I'm not going to spend my time and most important energy chasing her down. There's nothing I can do."

"Rose, I know it's YOUR dog."

"Thanks for letting me know, but she is not MY dog. I met her just two weeks ago. Goodbye."

Minutes later, Rose stepped out the door, looked at the dog's water and food bowls, blankets and empty tether. In only a short time Rose was attached. She tried really hard not to care, but it was useless.

Later the same day, the phone rang. It was Beth. Her stern, forceful and anxious voice stammered in anger, "Your dog attacked my sheep and did serious damage to their ears. Joe shot at her. She ran off. She may be dead or seriously injured. We don't know. She will be very bloody. Joe saw blood droppings on the ground in the direction of her travel. Put that dog down if she returns. She's a menace to the neighborhood!"

Rose's heart fell. With little to say that could even come close to the devastation she felt, she responded in empathy and compassion, "Beth, that's horrible. I'm so sorry to hear that."

Beth slammed down the receiver. Rose flinched and set her receiver in its cradle. She stood up and lifted her throbbing chest.

Rose paced back and forth as far as her house allowed. It was not her choice to have Annie put down or if asked, pay for the damage she had inflicted on her neighbor's sheep. Rose had absolutely no idea that that dog was capable of such an act.

She had to call her friend and animal lover Sable, to share her dilemma. Her response, "You are the last place Annie had any kind of care. She'll be back," soothed Rose's shaky conscious.

For forty-eight hours Rose hoped and prayed that Sable was right.

It was a brisk rainy night. Rose and her white long haired cat Lily were cuddled together on the couch listening to the big rain drops hammering on the tin roof. With a start, Lily moved away, crept over to the multi-paned front door and peered out the bottom pane. Rose followed her lead.

To Rose's pleasure and surprise it was Annie, wet and shaking. Rose slipped out the door and plodded her way to the misplaced dog. Annie allowed her to take hold of her collar and bring her in.

The difficulties Beth had projected onto the situation dissipated. Annie had cleaned herself well. From the corner of her eyes she watched every move Rose made. When Rose wrapped a towel around Annie's torso and rubbed her dry her body softened. Rose looked her over. Relieved beyond measure, all she found was a nickel sized graze about a half-inch deep. Only inches away from a fatal wound, the bullet hit the top of the inside of her front right leg. Rose was shocked to be able to see the untouched leg to chest artery pumping blood.

Rose applied some antiseptic cream to Annie's injury and wrapped it in gauze. Then took her by the collar, tethered her to the porch. Annie had found her refuge. She went fast to sleep.

Calling Beth to let her know Annie had arrived home, Rose hoped that she could bring a little peace of mind to her neighbor. But before she got the chance to say anything Rose stated, "I promise I will never allow my dog to leave my property unless I am with her. I can, if you'd like, help with the care of your sheep. Because I didn't know Annie was capable of attacking sheep I don't feel responsible for the vet bill."

But Beth shouted out, "Rose, you just said MY dog. It is YOUR dog. YOU are responsible for its actions."

Rose was not going to give in. She pondered and then in an even tone repeated, "I didn't know she would attack your sheep. If I did I wouldn't have allowed her to leave my property under any circumstances unless I was with her."

It took only a few days for Beth and Joe to accept Rose's help.

Rose did what she was allowed and what she could, but a discomfort penetrated all that she did.

It warmed Rose's heart when one day Joe said with the sincerity she knew to be true of him, "Rose if I knew it was your dog I would have never shot at it. I would have shot above its head and then called you. I'm sorry."

Torn, hurt and frustrated Rose had to remove her self-imposed responsibilities. Her focus needed to be on her dog Annie, not the sheep.

After only a week's time, Annie's wound healed nicely. Their training resumed. Annie still needed to understand the rules of Rose's home, her name and accept the security Rose had to offer her.

A second trip to the vet was in order. Annie loaded into and rode in the car like a pro. Their wait was short. Without a snip or a growl Annie let the vet check her. Rose was proud. Her stomach showed no signs of birthing. They agreed that she had been spayed. Her teeth had enough growth and wear to put her age somewhere between six to eight years old.

Forthcoming the vet said, "It's very hard to determine the age of a mistreated animal. The wear on her teeth may be from chewing very hard objects in need of nurturance. They're people out there who should be shot for how badly they treat their animals. I've seen way too many to be completely impartial anymore, but I keep my mouth shut. All I can do is continue doing my job and give the appropriate advice to all who care enough to ask."

Rose agreed.

She was worried Annie may have heartworms. She told the vet what she saw in her stools and what she had done. He supported her work and explained that the grocery store de-wormer would never completely rid her of the unhealthy amount of parasites that were plaguing her system. The vet took a blood sample and gave her all the needed shots. He prescribed a de-wormer. The results of the heartworm test would be available in ten minutes. Very grateful for the short wait Rose loaded Annie back into the car.

Within seconds Beth drove up. She slammed her car door and marched straight to Rose. Her arms were stretched forward with two plastic, empty medical bottles in her hands. She fixed her cold stern eyes on Rose and declared, "You should be paying for this!"

Rose stood firm and said nothing. From the corner of her eye she caught a glimpse of the vet meandering in their direction.

He politely acknowledged Beth and Rose, then stated a welcomed truth, "The result of the heartworm test is negative. You're lucky. It's a very costly and time consuming treatment."

In a split second, Rose jimmied herself into the back seat of her car. Her arms wrapped around her dog. She sank her face into Annie's fur then whispered into her ears, "Even though I was completely willing to go through the treatment with you, I'm so glad I don't have to."

Rose paid her bill. Days before she said all she could to Beth. Rose and Annie went home.

After the prescribed doses of de-wormer were completed, Annie's energy went up a notch. She was more carefree, calm and responsive to affection. But her reaction to the food Rose continued to offer changed. She'd sniff at it, cover it with imaginary dirt and then lay down. Annie didn't respond to all of her meals in this way, but enough to worry Rose.

Rose began experimenting with Annie's diet. But not until that spring when Karen, a classmate who had dogs of her own and had traveled to Alaska, did Rose find the answers she needed to bring Annie to her optimal health.

She showed Karen a picture of Annie. Karen identified her as a pure-bred Siberian husky. That same week, Rose's charming friend Roman, was visiting when Annie's dietary needs came to a head. He had his laptop computer with him. They looked up Siberian husky diet. They discovered that that particular breed couldn't stomach beef, soy, wheat, corn and other ingredients in the dog food Rose was feeding Annie. Dogs, like Annie, preferred salmon and fowl, foods found in Alaska, the land from which her breed comes.

Rose honored Annie's needs. She became the happy receiver of fresh cooked chicken, eggs or canned salmon with her acceptable dry food. To top it off, one day they were walking by her horse Lana, who was munching on a few carrots. Pieces had dropped to the ground. Annie snatched one up. Surprised and elated by her dog's enthusiasm, Rose decided it was time to add another choice to the dog's diet. It was a success. Annie's teeth and gums improved. She left her little carrot for last and then chewed it with relish.

Silly Annie not only had preferred dietary needs, but also a mealtime. Rose had continued to give her food three times a day, but far too often, she disregarded the food. Ants, flies and meat bees covered and ate it, making the food inedible. With trial and error, Rose came to see that Annie's preferred time to dine was in the evenings.

Months had passed since Annie was witnessed attacking sheep and understandably shot at. Her life is calm, safe and protected. She is a quiet, at times aloof, beautiful girl who has settled into Rose and her other fine furry friends' routine.

Annie speaks in a tenor's howl so infrequently that the immediate neighbors hardly know she's around. Not long after breakfast, Rose and Annie take a brisk walk. A real trooper on the leash she has upped Rose's pace. When they get home she waits for her to tell her to "sit" outside the front door and then when she has settled a bit she is allowed to rush to her spot. Without a word from Rose, she lies down on her bed right next to Rose's writing station.

Eventually, when she walks to the front door needing to go outside, Rose happily responds. She attaches Annie's leash to her. They stroll around the property and then back to her spot on the porch.

Annie's winter coat is gone and shortly she will get her first bath.

Rose believes Joe and Beth's words, "We are happy Annie is doing so well."

A lightweight metal collar with I.D. tags surrounds Annie's neck. The heaviness of the thick metal collar she wore when Rose met her is a part of their history. Rose let go of the fears she had for Annie's safety. She has made friends in their neighborhood. Annie has a home. Her eyes sparkle.

Annie's first anniversary with us arrived. She was an essential part of our lives.

The weather report announced, "Snow is not expected to arrive in our region until midnight."

A determined Rose figured, "I'll be back before nightfall. No problem."

She donned long johns, a wool sweater, blue jeans, high-top leather boots, wool gloves and a coat. Excited to share her newest piece, she loaded up her writing materials and then stuffed her purse into her black nylon backpack, put some firewood into her cast-iron stove and shut it down. She hurried outside, fed Lana, drove the two miles to the corner and then parked Sammy at the bus stop.

Rain-filled clouded skies canopied the fifteen-mile bus ride that snaked down and up the river canyon. After making one connection she arrived just in the nick of time, 2pm.

Rose rushed into the classroom, sat down and attempted to focus on the lecture. It was impossible. Students were poking their elbows into each other's arms. Nervous murmurs and heads shook, sucking the air right out of the room. Unbeknownst to her, while she was securely riding though the lush evergreen shrub, oak and pine tree landscape, the weather report had changed. Big beautiful flakes of white snow filled the sky. At 3:15 pm the class was canceled.

Panic oozed its way into Rose's thoughts. "I wish I'd stayed home."

She had befriended a few ladies in the class.

Glancing around the room Rose couldn't help but hope, "Who out of all these people would be generous enough to help me? Not her or him, maybe her."

She squelched her pride and then said to Karen sitting only a couple of seats away, "My bus ride home is going to be canceled. May I catch a ride to the library? It's only a couple of miles from your home."

Karen jumped out of her seat. Frantically gathering her papers and shaking her head she said, "No. I come from southern California and rarely drive in the snow. I'm worried about the two miles that I have to drive just to get myself home. Sorry."

Rose's thoughts flipped from one idea to another, "Where can I spend the night? I have my debit card and some cash. Thank God! But how do I get to a motel or hotel, walk?"

Rose ran as hard as she could to the college's bus stop. Her thoughts focused on the slightest bit of hope, "Maybe it's still running."

Then she saw the creative writing teacher Sue, with her pal Bonnie, making their way to their car. Those two lovely ladies were supportive of her work in a diplomatic, forthcoming and honest way. Would they help? She held onto her integrity, but nonetheless could feel the pleading in her words, "As I recall, you both live near the library. If it's not too much out-of-your-way, could you please leave me off there. I'd really appreciate it."

Fearing rejection in the depths of who she thought she was Rose said to herself, "They don't know me. I don't blame them if they make up an excuse and say sorry. But we can't."

Sue and Bonnie looked down at the soon-to-be snow covered pavement. Silent, cautious seconds passed between Rose's question and their answer. In slow motion Sue turned to face Bonnie and then back to Rose to say, "It's not out of our way."

Bonnie nodded.

"Thank you so much!"

The whole way there carpets of snow accumulated on the sidewalks, lawns and rooftops.

Sue made the only small talk during that all important short trip to the library, "Rose, check out Julia Alvarez's, *In the Time of the Butterflies*. You'd enjoy her work."

Rose jotted down Sue's recommendation in her binder. It took her mind off her worries, but not for long. Logic was embedded in Rose's thoughts, "I'll bet all the buses will be canceled any minute. It's far too dangerous."

Sue and Bonnie stopped across the street from the library, "Good luck, Rose," and then continued home.

Snow, hail and wind pushed Rose hard toward the opening of the only sanctuary she had. The sign on the library door said, closed 5pm. It was closing in on 4pm. The bus home had been canceled. Rose was stranded. She needed to make a reservation at a motel or hotel in the area soon. An old classmate, Janet, now librarian, was behind the desk.

A politeness that hid her jittery nerves Rose came out with, "May I use the phone?"

"Yes but, I have an idea. Doris, one of our most trusted librarians, lives up your way. She's getting off in fifteen minutes and could use a co-pilot. She won't admit she needs help, but we'd feel much better if she had someone with her."

A soft spoken, vital women in her seventies with big brown eyes, wide shoulders and gray-streaked shoulder-length brown hair walked over to the desk, "Are you sure it's OK for me to leave?"

"Yes, of course."

"Doris I'd like to introduce you to Rose, an old classmate of mine. She lives in your neighborhood and needs a ride home. Could you use the company?"

She responded, "I suppose," and shrugged her shoulders.

With a sincere and reserved gratitude coming from her eyes Janet politely said, "Thanks, Rose."

Doris and Rose picked up their belongings, pushed through the library's front door and minced their way down the snow-covered stairway. As they approached Doris' gray Toyota truck parked in a lot across the street of the library, she pointed out the mound of river rocks in the back-end of the truck bed.

Rose nodded and then took in a couple of calming breaths before responding, "Smart."

Doris started the engine and boasted, "I've done this before. We can make it."

Rose was grateful, but she knew she was in the hands of a seventy year old woman she had just met. She was fifty-eight and wise, but wasn't so sure how wise at that moment.

She pondered, "What kind of a driver is she?"

They headed for the freeway. Doris traveled through the hard-driving snow as if she'd done it many times before, assured and fearless.

Know-how permeated Doris' statement, "I don't have chains, but my tires are pretty new," all the while her hands clutched to the steering wheel, spine straight, chest open, eyes focused on the road ahead, attempting to reassure herself and Rose as they sped down a one-mile straight stretch of the freeway.

Panic seeped into Rose, "No chains! God help us."

Snow covered the road with light white flakes, except for one set of gray asphalt tire tracks. Rose was hopeful, but she knew she wouldn't have chosen to drive 45mph with the amount of ice and snow on the road. The weather accelerated in intensity, minute by minute. The snow clung to the windshield. The sporadic wind shoved Doris' little truck from side to side.

When they took the left hand turn onto the two-lane highway, fifteen miles from their destination, Doris lowered her speed to 20mph and downshifted to second gear.

Rose hung her head and prayed, "My life is in the hands of this woman. God! Give us the mental and physical strength we need, one step at a time."

They traveled another flat, straight stretch between the cross-roads and the County's government buildings down a long tree-shaded slope and then up again just outside the city limits. Traveling at the slow even pace of 20mph their lives shrunk as if in a slow moving capsule. A school bus passed them going in the opposite direction. Rose imagined the entire group of kids safe and sound at home. She assumed the next day would be a snow day.

If only for a moment, Rose was given the opportunity to think, "I wish I were one of them. I hope we make it!"

Doris held the car in second gear, but the worst of the drive was ahead of them. More and more snow fell from the sky as they drove curve after curve. Flurries of transparent crystal prism snowflakes accumulated and framed the lower edge of the wind-shield. The wipers struggled to give them the visibility they craved. The canyon protected them from the wind, but nothing else.

Rose was intensely aware of how much she had to stay calm, no matter what. Even if it meant holding her anxiety and fear in check to the point that she didn't know they existed.

In a slow monotone voice Rose said, "Doris, I think we'd be better off slowing down and shifting into first gear. That will keep us at a safe speed."

Doris glared at Rose from the corner of her eyes. Her face distorted into what appeared to be a childish arrogant rebellion, but she obliged. They were now crawling at ten mph.

Rose went inside herself, "Thank You! My God woman, what were you thinking?" She inhaled to then exhale deep and slow breaths.

Rose fought her desire to drive. Although she did appreciate the ride home she wished she'd gone with her first inclination. Wait out the storm in a cozy motel. It would have been so easy to call her neighbors to ask if they would feed her animals and then go to bed.

Pointed in the opposite direction on the other side of the road, Rose saw what looked like Seth's car in the ditch. There was no one nearby waving for help, no footprints and no head popping out of the window.

A little prayer crossed Rose's mind, "Seth, I'd stop if I could. Be OK, at home, safe and sound."

For five miles they'd been able to hang onto the cliff-side of the long, windy road. But then the truck began a steady downward slide into the middle of the road, a side-angle descent toward the wrong side of the road and possibly down into the ravine.

Doris' right leg lifted ever so slightly toward the BRAKE, and at that very moment she started to turn the steering wheel AWAY from the slide. Rose knew putting the brakes on and or steering away from the slide was the last thing Doris should do.

Rose said in a firm, but soothing voice, "Doris, turn into the slide, Doris don't brake, don't brake, turn into the slide, turn into the slide."

Doris resisted the strong desire to press down on the brakes. With pinpoint focus and will she clutched her hands even harder around the resisting steering wheel and turned the wheels into the slide. The truck regained traction.

In truth Rose said, "Well done."

After gaining her equilibrium, Doris shared, "Thanks for saying something. I knew I shouldn't, but it's so damn easy to push down on the brake pedal and turn toward the direction I wanted to go."

Feeling assured and very proud of Doris, Rose said, "We're a good team, you and I. We'll make it home."

Laughing inside, Rose thought, "We maybe a couple of old broads, but we're not dead yet."

They continued the arduous process of getting home through the snow-packed road and puffy white landscape, following any vehicle tracks they were lucky enough to come across.

Rose needed to let loose of what was holding her hopes and wishes for their safe trip home intact. She moved her fixation of the road ahead and looked at Doris, "I need to let you know why I'm so quiet. It's because I've been praying. I haven't stopped praying since the moment we met. We need all the help we can get."

Doris didn't respond, nonetheless it helped Rose to just say it.

They passed under a group of, weighted down with snow, oak trees. If for only a moment, they traveled over mercifully bare pavement. As they approached the river's bridge at the bottom of the canyon Doris automatically shifted into second gear. The truck fishtailed. In the womb of the cab Rose and Doris rocked back and forth.

Rose's entire body stiffened. She clenched her jaw. The taste of intestinal bile inched up her throat and coated her tongue.

She screamed inside, "What the hell are you doing? We're going to plow right into the embankment."

Doris downshifted to first gear and then whispered in quiet doubt, "I've never driven this road when it's snowing at the bottom of the canyon." Edging up the canyon, they cut through a half-foot of snow which Doris' little chain-less truck was not equipped for. They were less than five miles from Doris' home when she announced, "If I'm not home soon I bet my daughter comes out looking for me."

Rose responded, "Good to hear," but prayed that they wouldn't end up in a ditch waiting for her daughter or meet her on the road, to then abandon Doris' truck, vulnerable to fallen trees, the snow plough or vandalism.

They continued, still in first gear, until the long easy curve right before and past Dave's Feed Store. The road widened. The danger of falling down a ravine ended. Now only one mile from Doris' driveway, the road sign, power-poles and tall trees poked out of the rolling mounds of three-foot drifts. At least a foot of snow covered the vague roadway.

It was not easy for Doris to say, but she did tenuous and fearing for her life, "This section of the road can get pretty bad. It's a slow upward incline all the way to my driveway. The heavy snow can sneak up on you. We'll never make it unless we speed up."

With the determination and will that she knew Doris needed Rose responded, "Go for it!"

Any semblance of a road had been engulfed with snow. Only mounds of snow-covered shrubs, fences, tall trees and mailboxes gave them any indication of where the road and Doris' driveway were. Doris plowed through the thick heavy snow. They fishtailed, almost hit a mail stand and avoided getting stuck in three-foot drifts or dipping into a ditch before spotting her driveway. Doris took a calculated left-hand turn, aimed directly for her driveway and succeeded. Snow had almost completely covered the tracks going up to her house. A welcomed shallow indentation led the way to their goal.

As they made their way up Doris' driveway she shared a bit of her world, "Three families live past my place. I'll bet they've made it home by now. My daughter lives next door. With any luck, she didn't go looking for me."

Her driveway made an even slope to a narrow bridge-covered creek. She directed her truck straight over the bridge. Out of habit, from the inside of her truck Doris ignited her electric gate. It stuck on a mound of snow. The gate started fanning back and forth, over and over again. They could see her house up ahead.

It was Doris' call, but Rose couldn't help but think, "If I were driving, a younger woman and alone, I'd get out and walk."

Doris shook her head then let out, "Shit! I shouldn't have done that. Now it won't turn off. I can't put it into manual mode unless it turns itself off."

It stopped. Rose asked if she could kick the snow out of the way and then open the gate, but Doris declared, "It can be tricky. I'd better do it."

Rose waited and watched.

After pushing the right button, kicking and shoving the snow out of the way Doris worked the gate open.

Rose thought, "This woman, a woman that I have just met is one independent, strong-minded, tough human being."

They passed Doris' daughter's little cabin. Her truck was parked nearby. She had made tire tracks up to Doris' house and the lights were on.

Doris sighed. Her essences said we're safe now. "My daughter will be glad I'm home."

A modest house, built by Doris' deceased husband welcomed them. A plush wine corduroy couch and matching chairs cornered the south side of the living room. Burgundy throw pillows accented the hearth of the wood-burning stove. A turquoise and wine wool Navajo rug that lay on a redwood floor centered the room.

Doris' daughter had been pacing the floor, making calls, worrying and as expected, was about to leave and look for her mother. Frozen stiff, Rose placed herself in the living room and then warmed her entire body near the fireplace. The daughter cornered Doris in the kitchen.

Rose couldn't help but overhear Doris' daughter stating what she knew to be true of her mother, "Why is she here? Why do you get involved with other people's problems? Did she talk you into driving her home? You should have stayed in town. You could of! What are we going to do with her?!"

Caught in the web of a foreign living room Rose feared for her safety. "Is her daughter mad at me for just being here? Or could it be the hours of worry for her mother's safety that's causing her to speak with such anger. What am I supposed to do? Stay if asked. Not likely. Walk out to the road and hike. I can't walk five miles. Should I call my neighbors to feed my animals or come get me? They work at night. They're not home."

Rose wasn't one of those people who misused others, but they didn't know that. Choices had to be made and fast.

Doris stepped into her living room. Rose sat cold and weary. Fulfilling her position as head of household, firm, in body and words Doris said, "Have you decided whether or not you are going to call someone?"

"No."

"My neighbor Gary has a 4-wheel-drive hatchback. It's great in the snow. He's a retired PG&E guy and would, more than likely, be willing to take you home, how about it?"

"Great, thanks."

"I'll call him. I got you into this mess. I'm coming along. I need to make sure you get home. Gary drinks in the evenings. He's probably had a few."

It stopped snowing. Rose and Doris trudged through the wet slush and met Gary at the end of the driveway.

They made it to the road. It was plowed.

Rose and Doris sang out in unison, "It didn't look like this a half-hour ago."

Whoever plowed the road was their hero. When they arrived at the turn-off Rose's snow-covered car was still parked near the bus stop. A silent prayer that no one damage or thief of her car comes to pass overnight soothed her.

For a mile, they traveled the well-driven country road with no problems. But as soon as they saw the spot that began a steep curved incline Rose insisted, "Gary, leave me off at the next corner. Fifteen years ago during a snow storm, I ended up in a ditch only a quarter-mile up the road. Ever since, on nights like this, I've parked and walked the last mile home. If we go much further the potential of you getting stuck, sliding downhill into a ditch and having to call for a tow-truck is high, even in a 4-wheel drive. Trust me."

"OK. I'll take your word for it."

Doris insisted, "Call me as soon as you get home!"

"I promise. I hope live coals are smoldering in the stove. Thanks so much for the ride."

Rose pulled her backpack out of the back seat. Her emotional energy was spent. The one mile between her and her home must be done on foot. Over and over again she repeated in a whisper, "I'm strong and healthy. I can do this."

The blending of day and night gave way to twilight. It was as if Rose could hear the canon of music in its gradual change with different parts taking up the same theme. Darkness was closing in, but the overlap of light and dark surrounded and held her. She foraged through her backpack for a flashlight. Nothing. The moon's glow hit the white snow and reflected off the walls of the Manzanita bushes on both sides of the road. It was barely enough light to see the way home. In short brisk steps, she stomped up the hill. Not wanting to slip and fall down, Rose stayed on the heavy snow that was left in the middle of the road.

She had made it up two steep curves and was about to continue up a long, even steeper stretch of the road, when her legs burned with fatigue and the will to get home weakened. Her chest pounded hard and fast, crying out "slow down or I might stop." Rose didn't want to die. She dug into the core of her very being.

No one was more important to her than she was to herself. As she slowed down her gait her pulse followed suit.

Some neighbors were stuck in a ditch. The wife and a crying child sat in their van. The husband had hitched his truck to the van and was struggling to pull it out.

If for only a moment, Rose thought, "I can't stop. I barely have enough energy to get myself home." She did muster up the energy to say, "Good Luck," as she walked by.

Coming from the bowels of their dilemma they offered, "Thanks. Good luck to you."

The road leveled out. The familiarity of her neighbor's lighted homes kept Rose from feeling lost and alone. If she needed to she could knock on their door and get help, but she kept going.

When Rose caught sight of her road, the concrete in her gut turned spongy, calmed her nerves and erased the fear of death that was lingering. She had a quarter of a mile to go. Her house, animals and personal sanctuary were in front of her. The kitchen light was on and her old horse, Lana, whinnied. Her soul needed to sink into the very being of an old friend. She removed one of her wool gloves and then caressed Lana's warm inviting forehead. Rose was home.

The mishaps of the everyday brought out a little more
of the best of who I am.

May is upon her home again. The turtles are back to sun themselves across the way on the rocks extending beyond the crystal pond. It's an evening of promise. Although starting out like most, feeding the dog and cat and walking out to Lana's paddock to let her loose for grazing. This particular night Rose had an outing, her writing group.

In haste, she gathered her writing materials, zipped down the driveway and onto the road to the local grocery store for a quick snack.

The group went well. They all had work to share, advice to give and laughs to laugh.

Homeward bound Rose drove to the edge of her property, went inside, stopped and closed the outer gate. Her mind was full of the group's activities. Consumed with the need to let go of the mind chatter and go to sleep she only momentarily thought, "Why was the outer gate open?"

Around 6:30 the next morning, Rose rolled out of bed and descended the flight of stairs to the kitchen. The day was moving along per usual, but the answering machine's light was blinking. Perplexed Rose pushed the answer-received button.

"Hey Rose. It's Patty. I'm sorry to call you so late. But I think I saw your horse on the road. I hope you get this message. O.K. honey, bye."

Rose shook her head and then said to herself, "She must still be here! It can't be Lana."

Her neighbors had said, "Lana's old, and even if you do forget to close the gate she wouldn't leave. She knows where the food is."

Nonetheless, Rose couldn't help but think, "Patty must be talking about another horse, but it could be her!"

Determined to get to the root of her fears, Rose threw on the bare essentials: tennis shoes with no socks, sweats and a coat.

She was far too anxious to eat, but she knew that she had to have some nourishment to muster up the energy to find and bring Lana home. Rose downed a glass of grapefruit juice.

Enticing molasses honey-covered grain in a bucket held in one hand and in the other Lana's halter and lead-rope, Rose began the mile walk to the location of her last sighting. Still in disbelief, she scanned the property and Lana's shelter, but no Lana in sight!

Praying that Lana had settled for the night in one spot Rose took hurried measured steps down her road then made the turn to Patty's place whistling and calling her horse's name every few yards.

Rose couldn't stop worrying, "Could she be somewhere else, down another road, up a driveway? Will I have to go back and get my car and look for her?"

Figuring Lana had been out at least twelve hours by then. Rose wasn't sure what to do except to continue the search with hope.

As she approached the area where her neighbor Tari's quarter horses lived, Rosie, a roan white faced mare and General Lee, a pitch black gelding, Rose sighted horse manure on the road. It was a clue, but no Lana. How old was the manure? It was hard to tell in the cool damp weather. But now at least Rose knew she was on the right path. After walking a few more yards she saw another mound. Rose called and whistled as loud as she could.

Lana's familiar long loud whinny from behind Rosie and General Lee's shelter answered her hopes and wishes for her horse's safety. Lana ran full bore down Tari's driveway. Rose stood awe-struck as she galloped toward her. Lana looked like the ten year old flea-bit-gray dark gray mane and blond tailed high-spirited Arabian, Rose had befriended years ago when she knew she would be her one and only horse. Rose watched with amazement Lana's graceful, now white, mane blowing in the wind, flaring nostrils and chest muscles driving her ahead. Rose was consumed with the knowledge that she had ridden her with her Queensland heeler-Labrador mix dog Ufda, by their side for ten years twice a week, come rain or shine or snow when they were full of endless energy and curiosity. She'd been Lana's human mom for twenty-two years.

In a startling pull to a halt, within an arm's reach, she lowered her head and inspected Rose's offering. Molasses honey-covered grain, the best that money could buy for her dear old horse, was a part of her morning meal for the last five years. Whinnying, snorting and big eyed Lana was ready to dive right into the bucket that held the enticing delicious meal. But then she caught sight of the halter and lead-rope in Rose's other hand and knew her capture was Rose's intent. Lana arched and swung her head and squealed. She pranced around Rose with youthful folly. Near enough for her to be very aware of her horses' thousand pound enthusiastic, powerful body. Lana's excitement was refreshing, but Rose held on to her respect for Lana's size and strength and stayed clear.

From the other side of the fence, her friends, Rosie and General Lee, shared in the fun. They attempted to push down the fence with their chests. Necks stretched to their limits and slung up and over they were determined to get to the contents of the bucket.

After the horses settled down, Rose lowered the grain filled bucket to the ground a couple of yards from the fence. Lana gave in to the temptation. After she had a mouthful she lifted her head from the depths of the bucket. Rose wrapped the halter around her nose and buckled it securely to her neck. The old "trick" worked once again. She allowed her dearly beloved horse to have a few more mouthfuls before tugging her head out of the bucket.

Rose didn't want Lana to devour it all. They had to get home and the grain was Rose's only power of persuasion. Moreover she couldn't simply walk away. She thanked Rosie and General Lee for hosting Lana on an overnighter and gave each of them a handful of grain.

Lead-rope and bucket in hand, Lana and Rose began the mile walk home. Rosie and General Lee trotted into a gallop parallel to them as far as their fenced in enclosure allowed. Lana neighed her goodbyes.

Rose still had a lot of work to do to get her home. In order to keep her in the direction of travel, Rose had to circle Lana around her to then bring her parallel to her once again.

When Rosie and General Lee were out of sight and earshot, Lana continued to neigh the tale of her evening out and the sadness she felt in having to leave her friends. Walking side-by-side, Lana's bare hooves clip-clopped in a steady rhythm on the gravel road, Rose sauntered. Her tennis shoe covered feet didn't make a sound. She stroked her pals' neck. In a sweep of emotion, Rose sensed a calm acceptance filling Lana's spirit.

Once home, Rose lead Lana back to her paddock and unhooked her halter. After adding some carrots to the bucket of grain in her shelter she felt privileged for the simple knowing of such a sweet energetic animal.

A half-hour later, after Rose had settled into her day's routine, she looked over to see Lana lying down.

Rose's thoughts drifted to, "Now I need to call and thank those who helped me keep my girl safe on her fun filled escapade."

Lana gave me a partnership in life's journey that
no human could.

Russell built himself a house. Rose created the peace of mind that she cherishes. From time to time, they cross paths and smile in recognition that who they were for each other wouldn't be repeated, but...

Flesh Remembers What Her Eyes No Longer See.

End of May, full of rains, phone calls I didn't want to end.
Your words of knowing loneliness filled an emptiness buried.
Life in another time when we were children living next door with loving parents so our hearts need not fear so deeply.
We shared a need to find a secret, private life after feeling raw and exposed by others.
I can hear your car, you're coming down the road, you haven't called, but it doesn't matter.
I know your sound.
I'm sitting out in the meadow drawing a wildflower, its 3 pm hot, sunny and bright.
I'm hot shining bright sweating at the sound of you.
You were money empty then, but memories of abundance gave you a dignity from days gone by when money flooded from your hands with no question.
We speak little.
Our actions speak of wants.
We create our time together with touches, longing and opening of ourselves.
We needed each other then.
Your round moist lips licked through my silk floral dress that then fell away from places only you were allowed to see.
What you wanted from me I gave freely.
We caressed the faces of our souls penetrating beyond us to the heavens that are of another world, lost in the subconscious.
Years of unexpressed passion flowed through my hands onto your welcoming body.
Kisses until we fell asleep then awakened when you had to go.

Walking down my steps, the rain moved us together.

I sat behind you wrapping my arms around your waist and arms, hot flashes came over us.

Your silky hand touched my cheek.

It was a touch of love between us for us from God.

You needed to say goodbye.

I thanked you. You thanked me.

Then you were gone.

Your laugh, smell, eyes, hair and hands, all are forever with me.

I Could Not Tell

I could not tell the world of my needs.
Parents, friends, boyfriends, would they understand
could they understand, feel me odd,
walk away, never to return.
I surely did not know so I did not tell anyone.
Then the time came, the person and persons
came into my life that would accept me as who I
was, am and would like to be.
A flower blooming, before you and me.
After time the could not tell changed again and again
as year after year found a new me forming within
the walls of my body.
Story after story found itself within my mind
forming on a page to share the could not tell of me.
I found comrades in the telling, I found separation
in the telling and I found me in the telling.
There always will be a could not tell because not all
can take in the telling.
To pick and choose who to tell
finds self-respect as the choices are made.
When I found the freedom of a safe could not tell.
A trust when you know a friend could not tell a secret
because he or she is your friend forever.

The End...

About the Author

Rose Leuty lives in the foothills of the Sierra Nevada with her horse, dog and cat. She is an avid reader. Her favorite authors include Haven Kim, Paula McClain, Anna Randolph, Terry Ryan, John Steinbeck, Kathryn Stockett, Robert James Waller, Jeannette Walls and Tobias Wolff. All of whom contributed to Rose's style.

Made in the USA
Columbia, SC
16 May 2021

37446467R00141